ONE POT

VEGAN EASY & TASTY

Clara de Vries

151 delicious Vegan One Pot dishes. The Vegan One Pot Cookbook with many One Pot Pasta & One Pot Meals recipe. Healthy easy One Pot cooking also for children and families.

1st edition
2021
© All rights reserved
ISBN: 9798720916015

Table of contents

WHAT EXACTLY DOES "VEGAN" MEAN? 1
    GENERAL INFO 1
    WITH DIETARY CHANGE 5

WHY ONE POT? 5
    QUICK PREPARATION IN JUST ONE POT 5
    ORIGIN OF THE ONE POT DISHES 6
    STRUCTURE OF ONE POT RECIPES 7
    COMPOSITION OF ONE POT DISHES 8
    RULES OF ONE POT COOKING 10

EQUIPMENT 12

ADVANTAGES OF ONE POT DISHES 13

NOTE ON THE RECIPES 15
    ONE POT MAIN DISHES 16
        Recipe 1: One-Pot Pasta "Asian Style 17
        Recipe 2: One-Pot Chili sin Carne 18
        Recipe 3: One-Pot Pasta "Colourful Vegetables 19
        Recipe 4: One-Pot Pasta with Creamy Tomato Sauce 20
        Recipe 5: One-Pot Pasta with Thyme and Oregano 21
        Recipe 6: One-Pot Pasta with a Hint of Coconut 22
        Recipe 7: One-Pot "Potato Stew 23
        Recipe 8: One-Pot Pasta with Mushrooms 24
        Recipe 9: One-Pot Pasta with Spinach and Mushrooms 25
        Recipe 10: One-Pot Pasta with Kohlrabi and Peas 26
        Recipe 11: One-Pot Pasta Mediterranean Style 27
        Recipe 12: One-Pot Pasta all'arrabiata 28
        Recipe 13: One-Pot Pasta with Chickpeas 29
        Recipe 14: One-Pot "Gnocchi Pan 30
        Recipe 15: One-Pot Vegan Curry with Rice 31
        Recipe 16: One-Pot "Spaghetti Bolognese 32
        Recipe 17: One-Pot "Indian Curry 33
        Recipe 18: One-Pot Pasta with Vegetables 34
        Recipe 19: One-Pot "Spaghetti alla puttanesca 35
        Recipe 20: One-Pot Paste "Veggie 36

Recipe 21: One-Pot Pasta Mediterranean Style 37
Recipe 22: One-Pot Pasta with Spinach 38
Recipe 23: One-Pot Pasta with Spinach II 39
Recipe 24: One-Pot "Quinoa Bowl 40
Recipe 25: One-Pot "Paella 41
Recipe 26: One-Pot Paste a la Martha Stewart 42
Recipe 27: One-Pot Pasta with Broccoli 43
Recipe 28: One-Pot Pasta with Porcini Mushrooms 44
Recipe 29: One-Pot "Colourful Vegetables 45
Recipe 30: One-Pot "Pea Stew 46
Recipe 31: One-Pot Pasta "Cream Zucchini 47
Recipe 32: One-Pot "Noodle Stew with Vegetables 48
Recipe 33: One-Pot "Fruity Rice 49
Recipe 34: One-Pot "Asia-Pasta'" 50
Recipe 35: One-Pot "Asian Noodles 51
Recipe 36: One-Pot Noodle Stew with Coconut Milk and Spinach 52
Recipe 37: One-Pot Chocolate Porridge 53
Recipe 38: One-Pot Pasta with Cashew Cheese Sauce 54
Recipe 39: One-Pot "Spaghetti Liguria 55
Recipe 40: One-Pot "Spaghetti Catalogna 56
Recipe 41: One-Pot "Spaghetti Porro 57
Recipe 42: One-Pot "Spaghetti with Zucchini Ragout 58
Recipe 43: One-Pot "Carrot Pasta with Green Asparagus and Hazelnuts 59
Recipe 44: One-Pot Ratatouille Paste with Olives 60
Recipe 45: One-Pot Macaroni with Peas 61
Recipe 46: One-Pot Spaghetti with Asparagus Sugo 62
Recipe 47: One-Pot Vegetable Noodles Once Hearty 63
Recipe 48: One-Pot Vegetable Pilaf with Nuts 64
Recipe 49: One-Pot Quinoa - Bowl with Sweet Potatoes 65
Recipe 50: One-Pot Curry, Spinach - Millet with Mushrooms 66
Recipe 51: One-Pot Hot Taboule with Halloumi 67
Recipe 52: One-Pot Potato - Broccoli 68
Recipe 53: One-Pot Potato - Pumpkin 69
Recipe 54: One-Pot Chanterelle - Gnocchi - Ragout 70
Recipe 55: One-Pot Potato - Chard - Vegetables 71
Recipe 56: One-Pot Potato - Lentils 72
Recipe 57: One-Pot "Winter" with Chestnuts 73
Recipe 58: One-Pot Tajine, Vegetables and Chickpeas 74
Recipe 59: One-Pot Bean - Paprika 75

Recipe 60: One-Pot Green Bulgur with Beans 76
Recipe 61: One-Pot Fresh Vegetable Rice Pan 77
Recipe 62: One-Pot Colourful Spinach Rice 78
Recipe 63: One-Pot Carrot - Onion - Risotto 79
Recipe 64: One-Pot Mushroom Risotto 80
Recipe 65: One-Pot Breakfast Quinoa, Sweet 81
Recipe 66: One-Pot White Beans and Vegetables on Pasta 82
Recipe 67: One-Pot Black Bean Burrito 83
Recipe 68: One-Pot Sweet Potato - Coconut - Curry 84
Recipe 69: One-Pot Lentils in Tomato Sauce 85
Recipe 70: One-Pot Couscous Salad 86
Recipe 71: One-Pot Mexican Quinoa 87
Recipe 72: One-Pot Tomato and Herb Soup 88
Recipe 73: One-Pot Tomato and Pepper Soup 89
Recipe 74: One-Pot Creamy Potato Soup 90
Recipe 75: One-Pot Pea, Dill and Rice Soup 91
Recipe 76: One-Pot Vegan Breakfast Cereal 92
Recipe 77: One-Pot Gnocchi with Chickpeas 93
Recipe 78: One-Pot Mushrooms in Cream 94
Recipe 79: One-Pot Tomato - Coconut Noodles 95
Recipe 80: One-Pot Noodles Pak-Choi and Shiitake 96
Recipe 81: One-Pot Pasta with Peppers, Vegan Feta and Walnuts 97
Recipe 82: One-Pot Pasta with Fennel and Saffron 98
Recipe 83: One-Pot Vegetable Pasta Green with Lemon Sauce 99
Recipe 84: One-Pot Pasta with Artichokes 100
Recipe 85: One-Pot Plum Pasta, Sweet with Poppy Seeds 101
Recipe 86: One-Pot Apple-Nut Penne with Raisins 102
Recipe 87: One-Pot Pasta TexMex with Avocado Salsa 103
Recipe 88: One-Pot Pasta Carrot Sage 104
Recipe 89: One-Pot Pasta with Peas and Mint 105
Recipe 90: One-Pot Penne with Rutabaga and Peas 106
Recipe 91: One-Pot Pasta with Vegan Feta, Pear and Chard 107
Recipe 92: One-Pot Wholemeal Noodles with Pumpkin Curry Sauce 108
Recipe 93: One-Pot Red Cabbage Pasta 109
Recipe 94: One-Pot Vegan Feta with Eggplant and Mint 110
Recipe 95: One-Pot Pasta with Tomatoes, Olives and Artichokes 111
Recipe 96: One-Pot Rice Curry with Vegetables, Pineapple and Peanuts 112
Recipe 97: One-Pot Kale - Rice - Pot 113
Recipe 98: One-Pot Curry Rice, Spicy with Beans 114

Recipe 99: One-Pot Millet with Herbs and Green Asparagus 115
Recipe 100: One-Pot Chard Bulgur Eggplant & Pomegranate 116

SPREAD 117

Recipe 101: Almond Puree 118
Recipe 102: Nut spread 118
Recipe 103: Jam Without Sugar 119
Recipe 104: Apricot Jam 119
Recipe 105: Date Cream 120
Recipe 106: Peanut Puree 120
Recipe 107: Hummus with Avocado 121
Recipe 108: Coconut-Banana Spread 121
Recipe 109: Jerusalem Artichoke Tuber Spread 122

BREAD 123

Recipe 110: Chia Spelt Bread 124
Recipe 111: Farmhouse bread 124

SNACKS 125

Recipe 112: Sheet Pan Kale Crisps 126
Recipe 113: Vanilla Cinnamon Almond Snack 126
Recipe 114: Hummus with Vegetable Sticks 127
Recipe 115: Sesame Sunflower Crackers 127
Recipe 116: Cinnamon Crispy Flakes 128
Recipe 117: Vegan Porridge with Vanilla 128
Recipe 118: Vegan Strawberry Banana Smoothie 129
Recipe 119: Raspberry Smoothie 129
Recipe 120: Breakfast Smoothie 130
Recipe 121: Vegan Pick-Me-Up Smoothie 130
Recipe 122: Good Morning Soup 131
Recipe 123: Quick Semolina Porridge 131

DESSERT 132

Recipe 124: Coconut Semolina Porridge 133
Recipe 125: After-Eight Chocolate Cream 133
Recipe 126: Berry Semolina Porridge 134
Recipe 127: Banana Chia Pudding 134
Recipe 128: Express Dessert Chocolate Banana 135
Recipe 129: Vegan Raw Food Dessert 135
Recipe 130: Colourful Fruit Island 136
Recipe 131: Vegan Chocolate Porridge 136
Recipe 132: Waffles with Coconut 137
Recipe 133: Fruit Bar 137

EIS 138
   Recipe 134: Banana Ice Cream *139*
   Recipe 135: Melon Ice Cream *139*
   Recipe 136: Avocado Ice Cream *140*
   Recipe 137: Mango-Pineapple-Coconut Ice Cream *140*
   Recipe 138: Raspberry Banana Ice Cream *141*
   Recipe 139: Fruit Lollipops *141*
   Recipe 140: Kiwi Popsicle *142*
   Recipe 141: Capri Ice Cream a la Casa *142*
   Recipe 142: Berry Ice Cream *143*
DRINKS 144
   Recipe 143: Herb-Ginger-Spice Tea *145*
   Recipe 144: Infused Water *145*
   Recipe 145: Pineapple-Lime Drink *146*
   Recipe 146: Lemon Ginger Lemonade *146*
   Recipe 147: Peach Iced Tea *147*
   Recipe 148: Pomegranate Lemonade *147*
   Recipe 149: Cucumber-Mint Lemonade *148*
   Recipe 150: Strawberry and Rosehip Iced Tea *148*
   Recipe 151: Orange-Lemon Iced Tea *149*

CLOSING WORDS **150**

What Exactly Does "Vegan" Mean?

General Info

Clarification of terminology

First of all, I would like to shed some light on the terminology and thus the origin and meaning.

Veganism, which is the term for the vegan lifestyle, actually emerged from vegetarianism. In the mid-1940s, the term was reinvented as a logical consequence of vegetarianism. At the beginning of the 1960s, the term was also given a definition, describing the lifestyle of abstaining from all food of animal origin. In addition, there is also the increase of abstaining from other animal products, such as leather. In this form, these adherents also reject the further use of animals, such as animal testing. This has manifested itself more and more recently.

Motives

The motives can be of different natures, I will briefly outline them here, since it is actually supposed to be about the recipes, but as we all know, a little theory is not wrong either.

Animal ethics

Animal ethics has now found its way into philosophy. It is a discussion of the moral justification for inflicting suffering on a creature for whatever reason. Unfortunately, we inflict suffering on an animal when we as humans want to add it to our food chain. The discussion of whether an animal can feel suffering also plays a role here, which is also related to animal husbandry. So, it is not only about the "end product", but also about the whole way of life of the animal.

Environmental compatibility

What does veganism have to do with the environment? A lot, because keeping animals for meat production has an impact on global CO_2 emissions. For one thing, land is needed, food is needed for the animals and biomass is produced, not to mention methane emissions. Basically, it can be said that more resources are consumed than the meat produced.

Feeding the world's population

Basically, it can be said that if less meat is eaten, then less land and resources are needed in terms of food for animals, which in turn could be used directly, in a better yield ratio, for food for humans.

Health aspects

Since animals have to be protected against diseases, a lot of antibiotics are used in agriculture. This in turn accumulates in the meat, which humans then consume. Excessive "ingestion" of antibiotics can lead to resistance to antibiotics.

Health consideration

Another short paragraph on the consideration of nutrients. With a vegan diet, the animal portion is logically omitted. This actually raises 2 questions. Do humans urgently need animal nutrients? And if so, can these be replaced by plant-based nutrients?

This is about the "normal adult". Pregnant women, children, competitive athletes and people with specific illnesses have different nutrient requirements and therefore often have a different nutrition plan.

Basically, however, one can say that there are 3 areas in the vegan diet, the non-critical nutrients, the potentially critical nutrients and the critical nutrients. In the literature, it can be traced that according to unanimous opinion there is a point of attention with the nutrients, iodine and vitamin B12. More attention should be paid to whether there is a deficiency here.

Personal reasons

Many see in the media, the treatment of animals, e.g. on the way to the slaughterhouse or also in relation to animal husbandry (such as the killing of male chicks, too little freedom of movement, etc.). Some animals are treated better, some worse. It is presumptuous to discuss at this point why this is, so, it is just a matter of pointing it out. Some people see this poor treatment as their reason for no longer wanting to support this and therefore give up meat and ultimately even all animal products.

Vegan food - delimitation

A legal definition does not exist, neither in Europe nor nationally. In the Federal Republic of Germany, a regulation of the Conference of Consumer Protection Ministers was issued in 2016, which is supposed to provide a definition, which can be read here. Vegan food is food without animal origin or additives, neither in the production nor in the processing.

Alternative food

The market for vegan food has grown strongly in recent years and therefore, there is an ever-increasing choice of substitute foods. Just briefly, for animal milk there is plant milk, for meat there are vegan products, meanwhile on different bases. It is no longer the case that people have to do without massive amounts of food, but rather that there is a variety that is worth looking at and the trend will go in the direction of even more variety. A small side note: you should still pay attention to the salt content of the food, which could be quite high in some cases.

Other forms of vegan diet

For the sake of form, I would like to mention other forms of vegan nutrition, but I won't go into them here. There is also the

- Organic vegan diet
- Frugal diet
- Vegan raw food
- High-carb diet
- Pudding vegan

With Dietary Change

When changing the diet, it is therefore important to ensure that there is a sufficient dietary mix so that there is no deficiency of vitamins, proteins or fatty acids.

As long as these points are observed, nothing stands in the way of a change. With this in mind, let's move on to recipes so that you have a sufficient selection of different meals.

Why One Pot?

You've probably heard of "one-pot meals" before, because this type of cooking is considered one of the modern cooking trends. And for a good reason, because the recipes are not only quick and easy, but also really delicious!

The popularity and familiarity of this food trend is not surprising, however, when you consider its origins. Strictly speaking, "one-pot meals" are not a newfangled trend, but the revival of one of the oldest and most widespread cooking methods. Since it has always been suitable for preparing delicious and substantial meals with little effort, even for many guests, one can understand why it has long proven itself in many kitchens. But how do "one-pot recipes" work?

Quick Preparation in Just One Pot

The term "one-pot" comes from English and means nothing other than "one-pot". So, this type of dish has existed in Germany for a long time, because even our grandmothers prepared nutritious, hearty stews. Overall, "one-pot dishes" can also be compared to the classic stew. This is because both variants involve cooking a base of cereal products or pulses with liquids, spices and vegetables in a pot to create a delicious meal.

Nevertheless, there are significant differences between the two dishes: The main purpose of a stew is to warm and fill you up. It usually consists of potatoes, cereals or pulses with vegetables or meat and is characterised by the fact that it has to cook for a long time. The end product is a wholesome soup. The variety of "one-pot dishes", on the other hand, knows no bounds: everything is possible via soups, salads, pasta, rice or potatoes! The aim is not just to fill you up, but the recipes place great emphasis on a simple, yet healthy and balanced diet.

Origin of the One Pot Dishes

The origin of the "stew" probably lies in northern Germany or East Prussia, as people there cooked over an open fire for a long time and did not have a variable cooking area or a closed cooker. This made it practical and necessary to cook different ingredients together in one cauldron. In addition, the stew played an important role in the First World War, as large masses of soldiers had to be fed at that time. For a stew, you could prepare large quantities and many different foods at the same time and thus feed many people.

However, this use of stews to feed the war soldiers led to the stew being considered a poor man's or peasant's dish for a long time. Later, under National Socialism, the stew became a symbol of community, equal and shared food, which was supposed to place national commonality above social differences.

This way of cooking together and then eating a nutritious and varied meal together from just one pot is probably thousands of years old. It is assumed that this cooking technique was known or is known in almost all cultural circles. Examples of this are the Roman cereal porridge, which contained pulses (e.g. beans) in addition to various grains such as barley. Or the North American hominy, which consisted of maize, beans and fish or meat. But even today, many cultures have stews, such as the Indian curry or the Japanese nabemono.

Nevertheless, "one pot meals" are considered a modern food trend, which probably first became known through the American TV chef, Martha Stewart. The US-American comes from New Jersey and works as an author, presenter, entrepreneur and cook. Her goal is to make everyday life and household chores easier and less stressful, but without sacrificing sophistication and style. To this end, she is always spreading great recipes or easy tips and tricks that significantly improve the household with little effort. For this reason, she is considered the "best housewife" in the USA, from whom one can learn a lot.

In this context, Martha Stewart was the first cook to spread recipes for the modern one-pot version, "One Pot Pasta". She used a tomato sauce with basil and pasta and cooked everything together in one pot. All in all, for a "One Pot Pasta" you prepare both the sauce and the vegetables as well as the pasta in one pot. However, since there are endless variations of pasta dishes, it is not surprising that this idea quickly spread and was varied. Moreover, this idea has been developed further and further, so that today there are no longer just recipes for "one pot pasta", but in fact a wide variety and possible combinations of different "one pot dishes".

This means that "One Pot Recipes" are not only instructions for nutritious soup or stews, but they offer a wide variation of ingredients, combinations and dishes, so that there are hardly any limits to the trend. That's why cooking according to "One Pot Recipes" is not only suitable for people who don't feel like or don't have time to cook, but for anyone who wants to try out new things or prepare varied dishes. This way you can delight yourself, your whole family or your friends with a great meal!

Structure of One Pot Recipes

Basically, every "One Pot recipe" works the same way: the idea is to put different ingredients in a pot one after the other and cook them together to get a varied meal. Nevertheless, there are a few rules to follow, as not every dish can be converted into an "one pot dish". In addition, the choice of ingredients must also be considered, as some things are more suitable than others. For this reason, the most important rules for ingredient selection, composition and preparation of "One Pot dishes" are described and explained below. In addition, these rules, quantities and procedures are automatically implemented in our recipes, so you can simply follow the instructions and procedures in the recipes to get delicious dishes from just one pot!

Composition of One Pot Dishes

A vegan "one pot meal" always consists of at least three ingredients: First, you need a base, which is the main ingredient of the meal. This is then supplemented with different vegetables. Finally, you need certain liquids that you can refine by adding herbs or spices. This means that "one pot recipes" also follow a specific structure. Therefore, it is important to select suitable foods to achieve the desired result.

Carbohydrate foods such as potatoes, rice, quinoa, millet, bulgur, couscous or pasta are particularly suitable as a basis for "one pot dishes". Alternatively, pulses are also a suitable basis. These include lentils, chickpeas and various beans. Tofu, which is made from soybeans, can also serve as a base.

The second important component for vegan "one pot dishes" is the vegetables. There are no limits to the selection and variation, so that new and exciting "one pot dishes" can always be created. However, there are types of vegetables that are better suited for preparation in a pot than others. This is because a short cooking time and a high variety of flavour combinations are particularly advantageous. For this reason, vegetables such as tomatoes, spinach, corn, mushrooms, broccoli, cauliflower, peppers, aubergine and courgettes are particularly suitable for use in "one pot recipes". Onions, garlic or ginger can also be used as flavour carriers. The advantage of these vegetables is that they can be combined with various spices, liquids and bases to create delicious dishes and only need a short time to become soft.

Finally, the choice of liquids, herbs and spices is crucial for the taste of the finished "One Pot dish". Depending on the selection, you can give the meal a Mediterranean, Asian, Latin American or various other flavour. This means that you can always try out new variants and variations and prepare varied dishes.

Therefore, you first choose a liquid in which to cook the base. This liquid also forms the basis for the sauce of the dish. You can simply and classically use water, but cream, bouillon, wine, strained tomatoes or coconut milk are also excellent for "one pot dishes", so you can use them flexibly according to your preferences and wishes. Then you should choose suitable spices and herbs to round off your meal and give it a special flavour. Salt and pepper can always form the basis to achieve a general seasoning. You can also add curry, paprika, oregano, herbs de Provence or many more to your dish. Alternatively, you can use fresh herbs such as basil, chives, parsley, rosemary or coriander and use them as you like. But tomato paste, cream cheese, feta, curry paste or soy sauce are also great for rounding off your "one pot dishes". As you can see, there are no limits to your creativity in "One Pot cooking"!

Since the selection and combination possibilities of "one pot dishes" are diverse and seemingly endless, we have compiled various recipes in this cookbook that will present you with a delicious result. This way, you can rely on our pre-selection and enjoy great recipes directly, without having to try out, modify and improve different variations beforehand. This cookbook therefore makes it easier for you to get started with "One Pot Cooking", but you can also take it to hand again and again to conjure up great dishes that you can rely on to be successful with little effort!

Rules of One Pot Cooking

Although "one pot recipes" are by and large clearly structured and easy and quick to implement, there are still a few basic rules that you should follow when cooking this way. Because there are some general procedures that are necessary for you to succeed with the "one pot dishes". For this, it is necessary that all the ingredients are added to the pot in the right order and that they are cooked for a sufficient time so that they are done. Therefore, the following rules can help you when cooking "one pot recipes":

These special features apply when cooking in a saucepan:

- Unlike large, flat pans, in which the heat is distributed evenly over the entire vessel, saucepans are cut rather high and have only a small contact surface on the cooker in proportion. This means that the heat is much higher at the bottom of the pot than further up. For this reason, you should put the basic ingredients, such as rice, pasta or potatoes, in the pot first, so that they get enough heat and become cooked.

- Moreover, when cooking in a pot, it is necessary to stir again and again. Otherwise there is a risk that the lower ingredients will burn or stick to the bottom of the pot, even though the upper ingredients are not yet cooked soft.

- **This is what you should consider with the liquids:**

  - Although cream, coconut milk or strained tomatoes are suitable liquids for preparing "one pot dishes", you should always add some water. This is because the basic ingredients need a lot of liquid to cook. Therefore, although you should use water sparingly to achieve a creamy sauce, you should always monitor the liquid intake to ensure that all ingredients are cooked sufficiently.

- Using the right amount of liquid to achieve cooked ingredients but still creamy and non-watery sauces is a balancing act. That's why I always give you the right ratio of the different liquids in the recipes, so that your "One Pot dishes" are a great success.

- **These are the rules you should follow when preparing vegetables:**

    - "One Pot Meals" are meant to be an easy and quick alternative for you to prepare healthy meals with little effort. That's why my recipes are specially designed so that they require little work and cooking time. However, it is necessary that you cut the vegetables as small as possible. This way you can effectively reduce the cooking time and quickly achieve a delicious result.

    - Conversely, it is also important that the vegetables in your pot do not cook for too long, otherwise they will become too soft and lose their taste and consistency. For this reason, you should only add the vegetables to the pot when the basic ingredient has already cooked a little. You should also follow an order to add the vegetables with the shortest cooking time last. This rule is also included in my recipes, so you can easily follow the descriptions and instructions.

Equipment

In addition to observing these rules, the right choice of equipment is also crucial for the success of "one pot meals". Therefore, the most important basics for preparing delicious meals in one pot are described here:

Overall, the special feature of "one pot recipes" is that they can be prepared in only one cooking pot. This is why the pot is the most important and decisive basis for a successful realisation of the dishes. For this reason, when choosing a pot, you should make sure that it is big enough to cook all the ingredients together. There is nothing more annoying than cooking in a pot that is too small and cannot be stirred without some of the ingredients ending up next to the pot. So, don't underestimate the size you need and go for a pot that is too big rather than too small.

In addition, you need nothing more than a chopping board, a kitchen knife and a wooden spoon to prepare "one pot dishes". You need these things to chop the vegetables and stir the ingredients in the pot. It is also useful to use a measuring cup to add the right amount of liquid.

Apart from that, you don't need any other equipment to cook delicious "one pot recipes". That's why preparation is quick and easy and the amount of washing up afterwards is very limited.

Advantages of One Pot Dishes

In everyday life, it is often difficult to have enough time for a balanced, nutritious diet in addition to work, household chores, leisure activities, voluntary work and many other aspects. Besides, no one wants to spend hours in the kitchen after a hard day.

This is the biggest advantage of the "One Pot Recipes": They show you how you can cook delicious, healthy and varied meals with little effort. This means you can prepare nutritious meals even during stressful periods. But not only do you save time when cooking, but also cleaning up is really quick: because you only use one pot to prepare all the ingredients! This eliminates the need to wash various pots, pans and bowls and instead you can cook and serve everything in one pot and only have to clean up this one pot.

In addition, "one pot recipes" are also particularly well suited to everyday family life. This is because children often have different preferences than adults, so some parents cook several dishes at the same time to cater to all tastes. However, popular children's dishes usually consist of a base with sauce or vegetables, such as pasta with tomato sauce, and can therefore be prepared super as a "one pot dish". This saves you extra stress and effort.

But even if you basically have the time to cook, for example because you have invited visitors, one-pot recipes can be an advantage. They allow you to have less stress before your guests arrive, because you don't have to frantically use everything your kitchen has to offer. Instead, you gradually add all the ingredients to the pot and let it simmer slowly. This way you can greet your guests relaxed and with a clean kitchen! This way, you can concentrate on your guests and the conversations during the evening and stay as long as you like. Because I don't expect a messy kitchen afterwards that you have to tediously clean up late at night or the next morning.

In addition, "one pot recipes" are also suitable for people who don't like to cook or don't cook often. Because the parallel preparation, cooking and seasoning of rice or pasta, sauce and vegetables can quickly lead to losing track or feeling stressed. However, if you decide on a "one pot meal", this can't happen to you. Because you have enough time to prepare the ingredients step by step and put them in the pot one after the other, so you can relax and concentrate on just one thing and don't have to monitor and carry out several processes at the same time. This eliminates the annoying running back and forth in the kitchen and the probability of burning part of the food due to carelessness is also very low. Cooking is therefore much less complicated and more pleasant.

The preparation of "one pot meals" has a multitude of advantages for you! Whether you choose to cook this way to save time, to lighten the load of your daily routine, to try new things or to integrate delicious alternatives into your eating habits, "one pot recipes" are suitable for many occasions.

So please yourself, your family or your friends with delicious, varied and diverse "one pot meals" and save yourself the stress of cooking and the work of cleaning up afterwards!

Note on the Recipes

Before we start with the recipes, I would like to give you a few important tips on the structure of the recipes. As this is not my first cookbook, I already have good experience of what readers expect from a cookbook.

Why does this cookbook not contain any photos of the dishes?

Some readers wonder about the lack of illustrations of recipes in cookbooks, e.g. on Amazon. To forestall the wonderment, here is an explanation from me:

Cooking and guidebooks are my passion. In order to share my passion with as many people as possible, I try to offer my books at an affordable price. However, this concern is not feasible with colour photos in books, as the printing costs are doubled. If you add the shipping costs, this leads to an enormous increase in costs.

Especially in this book, the added value of illustrations seems to me to be very limited.

If you have ever cooked a dish from a cookbook, you have certainly noticed that your dish usually looks different from the picture in the cookbook. This is because the pictures are also intended more as illustrations.

Putting over 130 pictures in a cookbook is, in my opinion, not helpful and doesn't fill you up. I have therefore aimed for a variety of one-pot dishes to give you as much variety as possible.

As a bonus, there are also refreshing ice cream recipes and delicious lemonades!

ONE POT
VEGAN EASY & TASTY

Main Dishes

Recipe 1: One-Pot Pasta "Asian Style

Here's a one-pot pasta with an Asian twist. Quick to prepare, it takes about 5 minutes of preparation and 15 minutes of cooking time and you have a quick dinner.

Ingredients

- 2 onion
- 4 garlic cloves
- 2 courgettes
- 2 red peppers
- 160 g peas, frozen
- 500 g fusilli
- 3 tsp vegan red curry paste
- 500 ml coconut milk
- 800 g tomatoes (tin), pieces
- 2 handfuls of cherry tomatoes
- 2 tsp fresh lemon juice
- Salt
- Pepper

1. To prepare, peel and chop the onions and garlic. Wash the courgettes and cut into small cubes. Remove the seeds from the peppers and also cut them into small cubes. Wash the tomatoes and cut them in half.
2. When the preparation is ready, heat some oil in a large pot. Add the onions and sauté until translucent. This takes about 2-3 minutes. Then add the garlic, pepper and courgettes. Fry the whole thing for about 2 minutes.
3. Once this is ready, add the rest of the ingredients, except for the salt, pepper and lemon juice. Simmer everything together over medium heat for about 15 minutes. Please stir occasionally.
4. If you do not have frozen peas but canned peas, please add them a little later, otherwise there is a risk that the peas will become too mushy.
5. Two minutes before the end of the cooking time, season with lemon juice, salt and pepper, stir and it's ready. Serve and enjoy.

Recipe 2: One-Pot Chili sin Carne

Here's a recipe, a little heartier but very filling, with a Mexican flavour.

Ingredients

- 2 tbsp rapeseed oil
- 1 red onion
- 3 garlic cloves
- 1/2 tsp chipotle spice
- 500 ml vegetable stock
- 400 g tomatoes, canned, chopped
- 1 bunch coriander, fresh
- 200 g red kidney beans
- 200 g canned white beans
- 1/2 tsp salt
- 1/4 tsp coriander seeds, ground
- 1 tbsp Cajun spice mix
- 250 g sweet corn (can)

1. Peel and chop the onions and garlic. Remove the beans from the can and drain. If necessary, run them under running water again. Chop the bunch of coriander.
2. Heat the rapeseed oil in a pot, sauté the onions for about 2-3 minutes, then add the garlic. Now sauté for another minute.
3. Then add all the remaining ingredients except the sweetcorn. Now reduce the heat, cover the pot and simmer at a low temperature for about 1 hour.
4. After about 30 minutes, you can add the sweetcorn. Stir several times during the entire cooking process.
5. After about 1 hour, the chilli is ready and can be served. Enjoy your meal.

Recipe 3: One-Pot Pasta "Colourful Vegetables

Here is a one-pot with colourful vegetables.

Ingredients

- 250 g rice noodles
- Olive oil
- 1 onion
- 3 spring onion stalks
- 3 garlic cloves
- 1 chilli pepper
- 500 g green beans
- 4 carrots
- 1 L water
- 250 ml vegetable cream alternatively coconut milk
- 1 tbsp curry paste
- 2 tbsp. soy sauce
- 1 bunch of fresh herbs e.g. coriander, parsley or celery leaves

1. Peel and chop the onions, garlic cloves and spring onions. Peel and chop the chilli. Wash the beans and cut into pieces, approx. 1 cm long. Peel carrots and cut into noodles using a spiral slicer. Alternatively, just cut into strips.
2. Next, heat a non-stick pan with a little olive oil. Then fry the onion, spring onions and chilli for about 5 minutes.
3. After frying, add the beans. Sauté for a few minutes, stir occasionally.
4. Then add the rice noodles and carrots and fill up with water until everything is covered.
5. Simmer for 5 to 10 minutes until the beans and rice noodles are almost cooked.
6. Just before finishing, add the vegetable cream or coconut milk and stir well. Season and salt to taste.
7. After seasoning, simmer for about 5 minutes. Then serve and decorate with fresh herbs, a few spring onions and a few chilli strips.

Recipe 4: One-Pot Pasta with Creamy Tomato Sauce

Here is a recipe for 4 people with Italian flair.

Ingredients

- 2 tbsp olive oil, virgin
- 8 Dried tomato halves in olive oil, finely chopped
- 2 tbsp tomato paste
- 1 tsp paprika powder, sweet
- 1 tsp Italian spice mix (e.g. mix of thyme, oregano and basil)
- 3 garlic cloves
- 2 shallots
- 65 ml dry white wine
- 500 ml soy milk, unsweetened
- 400 g penne, uncooked
- 500 g mini Roma tomatoes
- 1 tsp sea salt
- 1/4 to 1/2 tsp chilli flakes
- 3-4 hands full of fresh spinach
- Fresh flat-leaf parsley, for garnish (optional)

1. To prepare, peel and chop the garlic cloves and shallots. Wash and halve the Roma tomatoes.
2. Now heat a deep pan with a little olive oil. When the pan is nice and hot, add the sun-dried tomatoes, the paprika, the Italian spice mix, the garlic and the shallots. Bring to the boil, stirring, until the tomato paste darkens nicely and also caramelises. At this point, the shallots will also become nice and translucent. This takes about 3 - 4 minutes. Then pour in the white wine. Continue to simmer until the liquid has almost completely evaporated. This takes about 2 - 3 minutes.
3. When ready, add the soy milk, uncooked penne, fresh tomatoes, sea salt and chilli flakes. Now bring everything to the boil, then turn the heat down to low and simmer, covered, for about 15 minutes. The pasta must be almost soft, i.e. the penne must be al dente, firm to the bite. Please do not forget to stir occasionally during the simmering, otherwise the pasta will stick to each other or to the bottom.
4. When the pasta is firm to the bite, simply add the spinach and simmer again briefly until the spinach is wilted. This takes about 1 minute. Then serve and garnish with parsley. Enjoy it.

Recipe 5: One-Pot Pasta with Thyme and Oregano

A one-pot pasta with simple herbs, but very tasty.

Ingredients

- 2 onion
- 1 clove of garlic
- 3 tomatoes
- 3 thyme sprigs
- 4 parsley sprigs
- 450 g spaghetti
- 900 ml vegetable stock
- 1 tsp oregano, dried
- Salt
- Chilli powder
- 50 g grated cheese, vegan
- 1 organic lime

1. Peel the onions and the garlic clove and cut them into small pieces. Wash the tomatoes and cut them into small cubes. Hold the herbs under running water for only a short time. Shake them off well. When the herbs are well dry, then pluck off the leaves. Keep a little of them to garnish the food. Cut the rest into small pieces and put them in a pot with the other ingredients already prepared. Now pour in the stock and season with oregano, salt and chilli. Put the lid on the pot and bring to the boil. Then simmer on a low heat for about 10 minutes. Remove the lid and stir occasionally. If necessary, you can add a little more stock. Meanwhile, cut the lime into wedges. Just before serving, add the grated cheese, season again and place on the plate. Garnish with the remaining herbs and the lime wedges. Done.

Recipe 6: One-Pot Pasta with a Hint of Coconut

This time with a fine coconut note

Ingredients

- 1 courgette
- 1 red pointed pepper
- 3 carrots
- 4 spring onions
- 500 ml coconut milk
- 500 ml spicy vegetable stock
- 250 g ribbon noodles, vegan
- 1 bunch chives
- 1 tsp salt

1. Wash, seed and chop the pointed peppers. Peel and chop the carrots. Wash and chop the courgettes and spring onions. Then take a pot and fill it with the vegetables, ribbon noodles, coconut milk, vegetable stock and salt. Heat the whole thing and stir. If not stirring, put the lid on and bring to the boil. Once boiling, reduce the heat to half. The cooking time is about 9 minutes. But please check the packet again. Meanwhile, briefly rinse the chives and chop them. Finally, season with the chives and season again. Enjoy your meal.

NOTES

Recipe 7: One-Pot "Potato Stew"

A good one-pot can also be made with potatoes.

Ingredients

- 1 large onion
- 25 g rapeseed oil
- 1 tbsp olive oil per plate
- 600 g potatoes, floury cooking
- 600 g carrots
- 1 bunch chives
- 450 g water
- 1 tsp salt
- Pepper
- 1 tsp sugar
- 2 tsp spice paste for vegetable stock

1. Peel and chop the onion. Peel the carrots and cut them into small pieces. If you like, you can also slice them. Wash, drain and chop the chives. Peel the potatoes and cut into small cubes. Prepare about 450 ml of vegetable stock. Now take a saucepan, add the olive oil and heat it. Add the onions and carrots and sauté briefly. Add the vegetable stock and potatoes and simmer for about 20 minutes. Season this stew with salt, sugar and a little pepper and blend coarsely with a hand blender. Just before serving, add the chives and refine with a dash of olive oil. Enjoy it.

NOTES

_____

_____

Recipe 8: One-Pot Pasta with Mushrooms

Mushrooms, the all-purpose weapon of mushrooms, always delicious.

Ingredients

- 350 g mushrooms
- 1 onion
- 1 clove of garlic
- 2 tbsp. oil
- 1.5 tbsp tomato paste
- 150 g oat cream
- 1 tablespoon vegetable stock powder
- 200 g spaghetti
- 1 tsp Italian spice mix
- 1 teaspoon paprika powder
- 4 E yeast flakes
- Pepper
- Salt

1. Clean the mushrooms, preferably only with kitchen paper. Then cut the mushrooms into slices. Peel the onion and garlic clove, chop the onion but press the garlic clove. Heat 2 tablespoons of oil in a saucepan and fry the mushrooms and onions for 10 minutes. Then add the pressed garlic and 1.5 tablespoons of tomato paste. Fry for 1 minute. Then add 325 ml water, as well as the 150 g oat cream, the vegetable stock powder and the spaghetti. Now bring the whole thing to the boil. When it boils, lower the heat and simmer at a low temperature for about 8 - 10 minutes. Do not forget to stir occasionally. Just before the end, add the herb mixture, paprika powder, yeast flakes and chilli flakes. Season with salt and pepper. Let it sit a little until the liquid has absorbed into the noodles, about 2 - 3 minutes, and the delicious meal is ready.

Recipe 9: One-Pot Pasta with Spinach and Mushrooms

Here is a slightly different version with spinach.

Ingredients

- 200 g mushrooms
- Spring onions
- 1 tbsp rapeseed oil
- 100 g wholemeal spelt pasta
- 250 ml Soy Cuisine
- 250 ml water
- 1 tsp vegetable stock
- 1 tbsp almond paste
- 120 g baby spinach
- Salt
- Pepper
- Nutmeg
- 30 g walnuts

1. Clean the mushrooms briefly, preferably rubbing them with kitchen paper. Then fry them briefly with the spring onions in rapeseed oil in a pot. Then add the noodles, the Soy Cuisine, the water and the vegetable stock and bring to the boil. Let it simmer for about 7 minutes, stirring occasionally. After these 7 minutes, add the almond paste and season with salt, pepper and nutmeg. Now add the spinach and simmer for another 3-5 minutes until the noodles are firm to the bite. Make sure that the sauce has thickened. Finished and ready to serve. Top with walnuts on the plate.

NOTES

Recipe 10: One-Pot Pasta with Kohlrabi and Peas

A one-pot with light vegetables.

Ingredients

- 500 g kohlrabi
- 100 g young onion
- 1-2 garlic cloves
- 3 tbsp olive oil
- 100 ml oat milk
- 100 ml vegetable stock
- 4-5 sprigs thyme
- 200 g peas
- 300 g pasta, gluten-free
- Salt
- Pepper
- Nutmeg

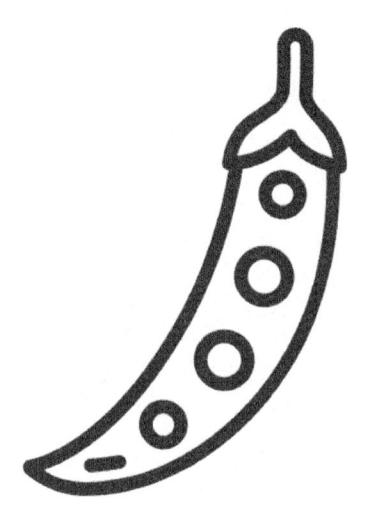

1. First, peel the kohlrabi and cut into approx. 1 cm cubes. Then peel and chop the onions and garlic. Heat the olive oil in a pot. Fry the onions, garlic and kohlrabi briefly. Then deglaze with 400 ml water, the vegetable stock and the oat milk and season with salt and pepper. Add a little nutmeg to taste and bring to the boil, but not too long. Now add the pasta and simmer for about 10 minutes, stirring occasionally. In between, pluck the leaves from the thyme and add them together with the peas. Bring to the boil again for about 3 - 4 minutes and season to taste. Serve when the pasta is al dente.

NOTES

Recipe 11: One-Pot Pasta Mediterranean Style

Would you like a One-Pot with a Mediterranean touch today?

Ingredients

- 250 g spaghetti
- 5-10 cocktail tomatoes
- 3 spring onions
- 1 jar chickpeas
- 1 can tomatoes, chopped
- 1 jar artichoke hearts
- 1 small jar of capers
- 2 tsp herbs
- 1 tsp salt
- 1 tsp pepper
- 1 clove of garlic
- 1 tsp chilli powder
- 400 ml vegetable stock

1. Wash and halve the cocktail tomatoes. Wash the spring onions and cut into rings. Peel and chop the garlic clove. Heat a pot with a little oil and when it is hot, add all the ingredients. Now bring the whole thing to the boil. Simmer for about 10 - 15 minutes, stirring occasionally. Taste to see if the pasta is al dente, then season briefly with salt and pepper and serve. Enjoy it.

NOTES

_____

_____

_____

Recipe 12: One-Pot Pasta all'arrabiata

Another variation with Italian flair.

Ingredients

- 2 onions
- 2 garlic cloves
- 3 to 4 chillies from the jar
- 400 g pasta, suggestion variety: penne
- 2 cans tomatoes, chopped
- 750 ml vegetable stock
- 2 tbsp olive oil
- 250 g date tomatoes
- 50 g olives
- Salt
- Pepper
- Basil, fresh

1. Peel and chop the onions and garlic cloves. Wash and chop the peppers (you can remove the seeds if you like). Put the penne, the chopped tomatoes, the stock, the olive oil, the onions, the garlic and the chillies in a pot. Heat the pot well and bring to the boil. When it has come to the boil, reduce the heat and simmer for about 15 minutes, stirring occasionally. If necessary, you can add a little more water. Wash and halve the date tomatoes. When the pasta is al dente, stir in the olives and the date tomatoes. Now season with salt and pepper and serve with fresh basil,

NOTES

_____

_____

Recipe 13: One-Pot Pasta with Chickpeas

A One-Pot for a giggle

Ingredients

- 300 g spaghetti
- 1 leek
- 1 aubergine
- 3 tomatoes
- 1 large pepper, red
- 1 piece celeriac
- 1 small tin of chickpeas
- 1 onion
- 2 garlic cloves
- 5 tbsp tomato paste
- 500 ml vegetable stock
- Salt
- Pepper
- some lemon juice
- Turmeric
- Oregano
- Thyme
- Basil

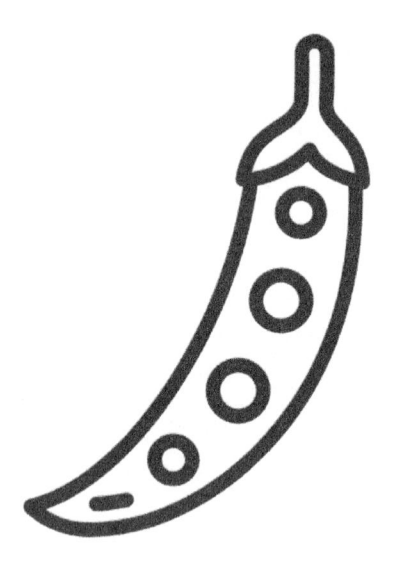

1. First wash the leek and cut into rings. Peel and chop the onions and garlic. Wash the chickpeas once and drain them well in a sieve. Wash the aubergine, tomatoes and celery well and cut into small pieces. Wash the peppers and remove the seeds. Then cut these into small pieces too. Put some oil in a pot and heat it. When the oil is hot, add all the vegetables. Add the spaghetti, tomato paste and herbs. Fill it up with the vegetable stock and bring it to the boil. When it boils, turn down the heat and simmer gently for about 8 minutes until the spaghetti is al dente. Don't forget to stir it so that the spaghetti doesn't stick. Finally, season with salt and pepper, add a little turmeric and lemon juice and serve.

Recipe 14: One-Pot "Gnocchi Pan"

Actually, it should be called One-Pan. But the pan is definitely delicious.

Ingredients

- 300 g gnocchi
- 2 tbsp olive oil
- 1 pepper
- 1 onion
- 8 cocktail tomatoes
- 50 ml white wine
- 50 g cream cheese, vegan
- 3 tbsp red pesto
- 2 handfuls rocket

1. Take some olive oil and heat it in a pan, preferably with a high edge. Fry the gnocchi in it. This takes about 5 minutes, depending on how brown you want them. Do not forget to turn them. Meanwhile, wash and chop the tomatoes. Wash the peppers, remove the seeds and then also cut them into small pieces. Peel and chop the onions. After the 5 minutes, add the tomatoes, peppers and onions. After another 4 - 5 minutes, deglaze with the white wine. Then stir in the cream cheese and the pesto. Allow to reduce to the desired consistency. To serve, add the rocket and arrange on the plates. Enjoy your meal.

NOTES

_____

_____

Recipe 15: One-Pot Vegan Curry with Rice

And here we have an on-pot with a slight oriental touch.

Ingredients

- 1 pepper
- 1 red onion
- 1 cup peas frozen
- 1 cup cauliflower frozen
- 400 ml coconut milk
- 1 tablespoon coconut oil
- 1 cup rice
- 2 cups vegetable broth from stock powder
- 2 tsp salt
- 2 tsp curry powder
- 1 tablespoon soy sauce
- 1 tsp. coriander
- 1 teaspoon hot paprika
- Garlic as required

1. To prepare, wash the peppers, remove the seeds and cut them into small pieces. Peel and chop the onion as well. Now heat the coconut oil in a deep pan at medium temperature. When the oil is hot, sauté the onions until translucent. Then add the peppers, peas and cauliflower, as well as the rice, coconut milk and vegetable stock to the pan. Bring to the boil briefly. Then add the soy sauce and spices and season to taste if necessary. Lower the heat a little and simmer until the rice is cooked and the dish has the desired consistency. Et voila.

NOTES

Recipe 16: One-Pot "Spaghetti Bolognese

An everyday one-pot that always succeeds, is quick to make and very popular.

Ingredients

- 250 g spaghetti
- 1 carrot
- 1 stalk of celery
- 1 vegetable onion
- 200 g veggie mince
- 1 tablespoon tomato paste
- 3 tomatoes
- 150 ml vegetable stock
- 100 ml red wine
- 200 g strained tomatoes
- 2 tsp dried Italian herbs
- Salt
- Pepper
- fresh basil

1. First remove the fibres from the celery and wash it. Wash and peel the carrots as well. Peel and chop the garlic cloves and onions, as well as the carrots and celery. Now take a pot, heat a little oil in it and let the veggie mince brown nicely. Fry the onions and garlic. After a few minutes, add the tomato purée. Let it roast for 5 minutes and then add the tomatoes, the stock, the red wine and the spaghetti. A little tip: it is best to break the spaghetti once in the middle. Now simmer for 10 minutes. Finally, add the strained tomatoes, herbs and season with salt and pepper. Don't forget to stir regularly. Enjoy it.

Recipe 17: One-Pot "Indian Curry"

...with an Indian note and slight spiciness.

Ingredients

- 500g potatoes
- 1 onion
- 3 garlic cloves
- 2 tbsp finely chopped ginger
- 2 tablespoons coconut oil
- 2 tbsp curry powder
- Pepper
- Salt
- 1/2 tsp garam masala
- 1/2 tsp cumin
- 1 large tin of tomatoes, peeled
- 2 small tins of chickpeas
- 500g spinach
- 1 can coconut milk
- 1 lemon or lime

1. Peel and chop the potatoes, onions, garlic cloves and ginger. Now heat some coconut oil in a pot. When the oil is hot, add the onions and garlic and fry until golden brown. Fry the ginger for about 30 seconds. Then add the potatoes. Now add the spices and fry for another minute. Then deglaze the dish with the tinned tomatoes. Cover the lid and let the curry simmer on medium heat for about 10 minutes. Please do not forget to stir. Then add the chickpeas to the pot and simmer for another 10 minutes. When the potatoes are cooked, add the spinach and stir well. Before serving, add the coconut milk and lemon juice. Now season with salt and pepper and the curry is ready to serve.

Recipe 18: One-Pot Pasta with Vegetables

Ingredients

- 2 portions noodles
- 1 small tin of beans
- 1 large tomato
- 2 carrots
- 1 portion broccoli
- Leek
- 500 ml vegetable stock
- Salt, pepper, chilli, garlic

1. Drain the beans. Meanwhile, wash the tomato and cut into small pieces. Peel the carrots and cut them into slices. Wash the broccoli and cut out the small florets. The leek is also washed and cut into rings. Now take a saucepan, heat some oil and when the oil is hot, add the previously chopped vegetables to the saucepan. Add the vegetable stock and the noodles. Let it simmer for about 15 minutes at medium heat and then season with salt and pepper, maybe add some chilli and garlic. And you are ready to serve. Enjoy.

NOTES

Recipe 19: One-Pot "Spaghetti alla puttanesca

Another one-pot spaghetti with an Italian twist.

Ingredients

- 1 onion
- 2 cloves garlic
- 75 g black olives
- 1 red chilli
- 100 g cherry tomatoes
- 1/4 bunch parsley
- 1/4 bunch basil
- 25 g capers
- 400 g chopped tomatoes
- 1/4 tsp black pepper
- 1/2 tsp dried oregano
- 1 tsp salt
- 250 g spaghetti

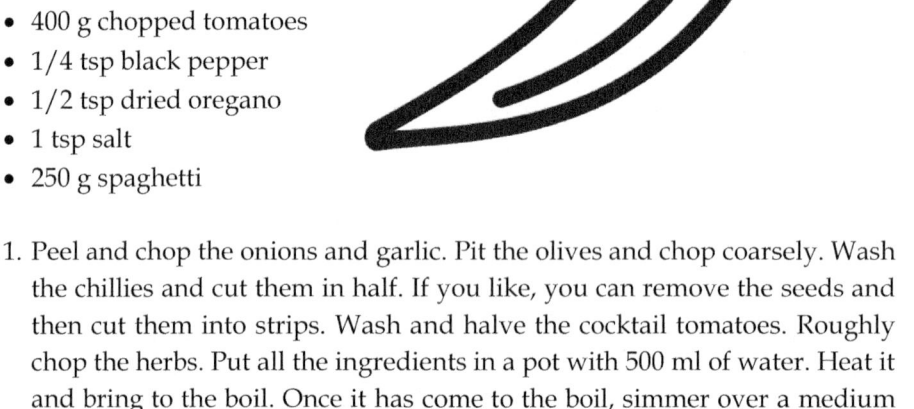

1. Peel and chop the onions and garlic. Pit the olives and chop coarsely. Wash the chillies and cut them in half. If you like, you can remove the seeds and then cut them into strips. Wash and halve the cocktail tomatoes. Roughly chop the herbs. Put all the ingredients in a pot with 500 ml of water. Heat it and bring to the boil. Once it has come to the boil, simmer over a medium heat for about 12 minutes without a lid. Do not forget to stir. After the 12 minutes, the dish is ready to serve and garnish with fresh basil. Enjoy your meal.

NOTES

Recipe 20: One-Pot Paste "Veggie

The name speaks for itself.

Ingredients

- 1 courgette
- 1 aubergine
- 1 red pepper
- 1 yellow pepper
- 100 g dried tomatoes in oil
- 2 garlic cloves
- 1 tablespoon olive oil
- 400 g pasta, farfalle
- 2 tbsp tomato paste
- 1 tsp salt
- 1 l vegetable stock
- 1 bunch chives
- 100 g feta
- Pepper
- Sugar

1. Wash the courgettes and aubergine and cut into small cubes. Wash the peppers, remove the seeds and the stalk and cut into small pieces. Drain the dried tomatoes and chop finely. Peel and chop the garlic. Now heat the oil in a pot. When the oil is hot, add the courgettes, aubergine and peppers and sauté. Then add the garlic and the dried tomatoes and sweat them as well. Then add the pasta, tomato paste, salt and vegetable stock and stir gently to mix everything in. Bring the whole thing to the boil and don't forget to stir. Leave the lid on and simmer for about 12 minutes over a medium heat. After 12 minutes, try the pasta. If it is still too firm, add a little more liquid and simmer until the pasta is al dente, continuing to stir. In the meantime, wash and chop the chives. Crumble the feta. When the pasta is al dente, season with salt and pepper and serve. Garnish the plate with the chives and feta and enjoy.

Recipe 21: One-Pot Pasta Mediterranean Style

...another Mediterranean-style One-Pot.

Ingredients

- 200 g leek
- 300 g pepper, red
- 150 g mushrooms
- 250 g tomatoes
- 500 g wholemeal spaghetti
- 900 ml water
- 300 ml oat milk or soy milk
- Salt
- Pepper
- 3 tbsp sage, finely chopped dried or fresh
- 5 tbsp paprika powder, sweet
- 3 tbsp. lemon juice
- 3 tbsp oregano, finely chopped dried or fresh
- 3 tbsp cornflour
- 100 ml water

1. Wash the leeks, peppers, mushrooms and tomatoes. Remove the stalk and seeds from the peppers and cut them into small pieces. Cut the leeks into rings. Cut the mushrooms into slices. Put these vegetables, the spaghetti, water and milk in a saucepan and bring to the boil. Once boiling, turn the heat down to medium and continue to simmer until all the ingredients are cooked through. Now season with salt and pepper and the other spices, stirring well again. After seasoning, add the cornflour mix to the pot and stir again. Now bring everything to the boil again and serve. Enjoy your meal.

NOTES

Recipe 22: One-Pot Pasta with Spinach

Simply with spinach.

Ingredients

- 50g onions
- 250g spaghetti
- 300g spinach
- 500ml vegetable stock
- 150ml Oat Cuisine
- 2-3 tbsp almond paste
- 20 g margarine
- 1 clove of garlic
- Salt
- Pepper
- Paprika powder

1. Wash the spinach well and drain or spin well. Peel and chop the onions and garlic. Heat the margarine in a saucepan. When the pot is heated and the margarine is hot, fry the onions until translucent. Meanwhile, bring the water to the boil using the kettle and mix the vegetable stock. Fry the garlic briefly and then add all the ingredients except the almond paste and spices to the pot and pour in the hot stock. Then add the noodles and simmer over a medium heat for about 15 minutes. Stir occasionally. When the noodles are al dente, add the almond paste and season to taste. Add a dash of cream at the end. That's it. Enjoy it.

Recipe 23: One-Pot Pasta with Spinach II

Another One-Pot with spinach. It's simply versatile.

Ingredients

- 400 g wholemeal spaghetti
- 3 garlic cloves
- 3 spring onions
- 2 limes
- 6 stalks basil
- 100 g vegan cream cheese
- 250 ml soy cream
- 500 g frozen leaf spinach
- 800 ml water
- Salt
- Pepper

1. Peel and chop the garlic. Then it's the turn of the spring onions. Wash and cut into small rings. Then wash the limes thoroughly and grate them with a kitchen grater. Wash the basil and dry with kitchen paper. Then pluck the leaves from the stems. Now put the wholemeal spaghetti, the garlic, the spring onions, the grated limes, the basil and the cream cheese, the soy cream and the frozen spinach into a pot. Heat the saucepan and simmer for about 15 minutes, taking off the lid and stirring all the time. Finally, season with salt and pepper and serve.

NOTES

_____

_____

Recipe 24: One-Pot "Quinoa Bowl

Ingredients

- 180g quinoa, red
- 2 garlic cloves
- 1 chilli pepper
- 120ml vegetable stock
- 250g canned corn
- 100g canned kidney beans
- 150g tinned peas
- 1 red pepper
- 1 avocado
- 2 tbsp tomato paste
- 1 tsp olive oil
- Juice of half a lime
- 1/2 tsp caraway
- Chilli powder
- Paprika powder
- Salt
- Pepper
- a few leaves of coriander

1. Peel and chop the garlic. Wash the chilli pepper, cut in half and remove the seeds. Wash the quinoa and drain in a sieve. Prepare the vegetable stock, but set aside, you will need it later. Wash the peppers, remove the stalk and seeds and cut into small pieces. Drain the beans, sweetcorn and peas. Peel and chop the avocado. Now take a pot and heat it with some olive oil. Add the garlic to the hot oil and fry. Add the chilli and tomato paste and fry briefly. When this is toasted, add the quinoa and deglaze with the vegetable stock and heat again. When the dish starts to simmer, add the peppers, together with the sweetcorn, peas and beans. The spices should not be missing at this stage either. Cover with a lid and simmer for about 20 minutes over medium heat. Finally, add the avocado and lemon juice and serve. Enjoy your meal.

Recipe 25: One-Pot "Paella"

Ingredients

- 1 cup rice, basmati
- 1 yellow onion
- 2 garlic cloves
- 1 chilli pepper
- 2 vine tomatoes
- 200 g carrots
- 80 g cauliflower
- 190 g courgettes
- 1 tin kidney beans (drained 255g)
- 150 g peas (frozen)
- 1 yellow pointed pepper
- 1 dash white wine
- 3 cups vegetable stock
- few saffron threads (approx. 1 tsp) (dried)
- 3 tbsp olive oil
- Salt
- Pepper
- 1 sprig rosemary
- some lemon juice

1. Wash, skin, seed and chop the tomatoes. Peel the onion and garlic. Chop the onion and crush the garlic. Wash the chilli, remove the seeds and cut into small rings. Wash and peel the carrots and cut them into half slices. Drain the kidney beans. Swell the saffron threads in 3 tsp warm water and set aside. Do the same with the vegetable stock, prepare and set aside. Remove the stalk from the pointed peppers, remove the seeds and cut into strips. Remove the florets from the cauliflower. Wash the courgettes and cut into small pieces. Rinse the basmati rice under running water until the water runs clear. Now take plenty of olive oil and heat it in a large pan. When the oil is hot, sauté the onions, chilli and garlic in it, turning the heat to medium. Add the carrots, cauliflower, peppers, kidney beans and courgettes. Don't forget to stir and roast the whole thing for about 3 minutes. Add the rice to the vegetables, stir again and deglaze with the white wine. Now let it reduce a little and pour in the vegetable stock and saffron water. Add the rosemary sprigs and bring to the boil. Then simmer on a low heat for about 10 - 15 minutes. Do not stir during this cooking time. Let's move on to the peas and the chopped tomatoes. Add them after this cooking time and simmer gently for another 5 minutes. Once the liquid has evaporated, the dish is ready and can be served with a squeeze of lemon juice. Enjoy your meal.

Recipe 26: One-Pot Paste a la Martha Stewart

Ingredients

- 170 g spaghetti
- 170 g cocktail tomatoes
- 1/2 onion
- 2 garlic cloves
- Salt
- Pepper
- 1 tsp oregano
- 525 ml water
- (Fresh) basil

1. Peel and chop the onions and garlic. Wash and halve the cocktail tomatoes. Heat a pot with a little oil. When the oil is hot, add all the ingredients and pour in the water. Bring to the boil and then simmer gently for about 10 minutes. Stir regularly. As soon as the spaghetti is al dente, you can serve it. Enjoy it.

NOTES

Recipe 27: One-Pot Pasta with Broccoli

Ingredients

- 500 g rigatoni
- 2 tsp curry paste, vegan
- 2 onions
- 1 l vegetable stock
- 100 ml soy cream
- 1 pinch of salt
- 500 g mushrooms
- 2 heads broccoli, small

1. First, peel and chop the onions and garlic. Then stir the stock. Clean the mushrooms, preferably with kitchen paper, and cut into slices. Then clean and cut the broccoli, dividing it into florets. Put the garlic, onions, mushrooms and noodles in a pot and heat or bring to the boil together with the broth. Simmer over a medium heat for approx. 6 - 7 minutes. Then add the small broccoli florets and simmer for another 10 minutes until the pasta is al dente. Do not forget to stir. Finally, stir in the curry paste and season with salt and pepper. Ready to serve. Enjoy.

NOTES

Recipe 28: One-Pot Pasta with Porcini Mushrooms

Ingredients

- 350g tagliatelle
- 450g porcini mushrooms
- 2 onions
- 2-3 garlic cloves
- 2 sprigs rosemary
- 1/2 red chilli
- 3 tbsp. oil
- 3 tbsp tomato paste
- 150g almond cream or coconut milk
- 3 tsp vegetable stock
- Salt
- Pepper
- Paprika powder
- Basil

1. Clean the porcini well and rub them dry, preferably dab them dry again with kitchen paper. Then cut into slices, thickness according to preference. 1 cm has proven to be not bad. Peel and chop the onions and garlic. Now wash the chilli pepper. If you like, you can remove the seeds. With or without the seeds, cut the chilli into small pieces. Wash the rosemary and shake dry. Neatly pluck the needles from the twigs and cut them into small pieces, or better, chop them into small pieces. Then heat olive oil in a large pot. When the oil is hot, add the porcini mushrooms and stir-fry. Add the onions, garlic, rosemary and chilli. Season well with salt, pepper and paprika powder. After frying, add the tomato paste to the pot. Sauté while stirring constantly. After sweating, deglaze with almond cream or coconut milk, depending on what is available, and about 800 ml water. Add the tagliatelle to the liquid. Simmer over a medium heat for about 25-30 minutes. Keep the lid closed. Stir from time to time so that the tagliatelle can absorb the sauce well and do not stick together. After simmering, season again and serve. You are welcome to garnish the plate with basil. Enjoy your meal.

Recipe 29: One-Pot "Colourful Vegetables

Ingredients

- 250 g rice noodles
- 1 onion
- 3 spring onion stalks
- 3 garlic cloves
- 1 chilli pepper
- 500 g green beans
- 4 carrots
- 1 l water
- 250 ml vegetable cream or coconut milk
- 1 tbsp curry paste
- 2 tbsp. soy sauce
- 1 bunch of fresh herbs e.g. coriander, parsley or celery leaves
- 200 g tempeh

1. To prepare, cut the tempeh into small cubes, fry in a pan until golden brown and then set aside for now. You will need it later. Please also check the package of the rice noodles. You may need to soak them in water. Then it's time to prepare the vegetables. Peel the onions, spring onions, garlic and chilli. If necessary, wash them as well. Then everything can be finely chopped. Wash the beans and cut them into pieces about 1 cm long. Peel the carrots too and cut them into very thin strips so they look like noodles. Put olive oil in a deep pan and heat. When the oil is hot, add the chilli, carrots, onions, garlic and spring onions and fry for about 5 minutes. Then add the chopped beans. Don't forget to stir occasionally. They should only be fried for a few minutes. Now add the rice noodles and carrot strips / noodles and also soy sauce and the curry paste. Fill up with water until everything is covered. Simmer for approx. 5 - 10 minutes until the rice noodles and beans are almost cooked. Then add the vegetable cream or coconut milk, depending on what is available, and stir well. Season to taste with salt and pepper. Now simmer for about 5 more minutes and serve together with fresh herbs. Enjoy it.

Recipe 30: One-Pot "Pea Stew

Ingredients

- 300 g peas, frozen
- 150 g red lentils
- 1 l vegetable stock
- 3 carrots
- 1 leek
- 1 potato
- 2 red onions
- 1 clove of garlic
- 1 tsp soy sauce
- Fresh chives
- 1 bay leaf
- 1 tablespoon olive oil
- Salt
- Pepper

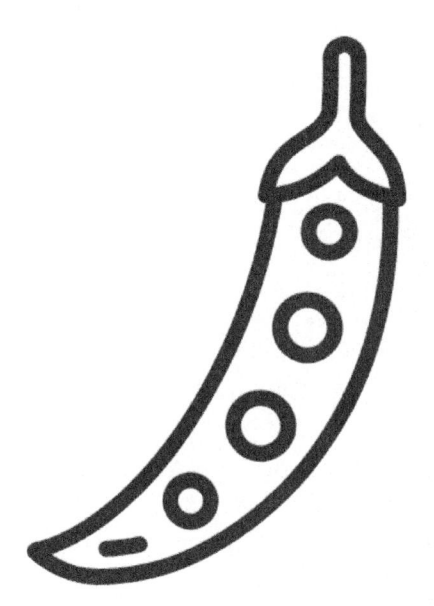

1. Peel and chop the onions, carrots, potatoes and garlic clove. Wash the leek and cut into rings. Heat the olive oil in a pot. When the oil is hot, add the onions and garlic and sauté until translucent. Then add the carrots and lentils. Sauté them briefly as well. Add the leeks, potatoes and peas. Deglaze with vegetable stock and add a bay leaf. Simmer everything on a low heat for about 15-20 minutes until the potatoes and lentils are cooked. Remove the bay leaf before serving. Now season with soy sauce, salt and pepper and fresh chives and serve. Enjoy

NOTES

Recipe 31: One-Pot Pasta "Cream Zucchini

Ingredients

- 500 g spaghetti
- 1 onion
- 2 tbsp olive oil
- 700 ml vegetable stock
- 300 ml vegetable cream
- 2 courgettes
- 1 tsp lemon zest
- 2 tsp salt
- 1 Msp pepper (white)

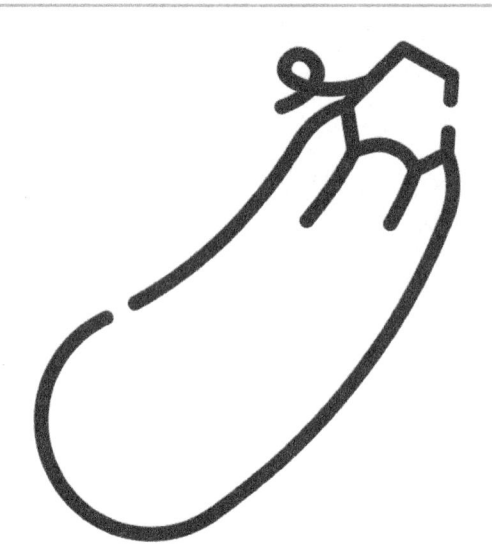

1. Rinse the courgettes well and remove the ends. Then roughly grate the courgettes. Then peel and chop the onions. Put the olive oil in a pot and heat it. When the oil is hot, add the onions and sauté for about 2 minutes until translucent. Then add the courgettes. Sauté for about 4 minutes and add the vegetable stock and vegetable cream. Cover the lid and bring to the boil. Once it has come to the boil, break the spaghetti in half and add. Simmer for about 7 minutes, stirring occasionally, taking care not to let the spaghetti stick. Before serving, add the lemon zest and season with salt and pepper. Enjoy your meal.

NOTES

_____

_____

_____

Recipe 32: One-Pot "Noodle Stew with Vegetables

Ingredients

- 2 tbsp olive oil
- 1 organic onion
- 2 tbsp tomato paste
- 2 organic carrots
- 1 tbsp. soy sauce
- 700 g organic tomatoes
- 700 g water
- 1.5 tsp vegetable stock, powder
- 250 g noodles
- 100 g spinach
- 1 jar white beans, pre-cooked
- Salt
- Pepper

1. As preparation, peel and chop the onions. Wash and peel the carrots and cut into small cubes. Wash the tomatoes, remove the stalk and also cut into small pieces. Drain the beans and wash the spinach. Heat the olive oil in a pot. When the oil is hot, add the onions and sauté for about 3 - 5 minutes. Then add the tomato paste and sauté for about 2 minutes. Then add the carrots, soy sauce and diced tomatoes. When all this is in the pot, pour in water, vegetable stock, noodles, spinach and beans and simmer over medium heat for about 8 minutes. When the pasta is al dente, season again with salt and pepper and serve. Enjoy your meal.

Recipe 33: One-Pot "Fruity Rice

Ingredients

- 100 g rice
- 150 ml water
- 100 ml orange juice
- 2 spring onions
- 1 pepper, red
- 2 tbsp rapeseed oil
- 2 tsp salt
- 1 Pepper
- 2 carrots
- 100 g peas, frozen

1. First clean the spring onions. Remove the stalk and chop the spring onions. Then wash them again thoroughly. Wash the carrots and cut them into small slices. Now heat some oil in a pot. When the oil is hot, fry the spring onions and carrots in it for about 3 minutes. Meanwhile, wash the pepper, remove the stalk, remove the seeds and cut into small pieces. Add the peppers to the pot and fry for about 2 minutes. In the meantime, rinse the rice with clear water and drain in a sieve. When it has drained, add it to the pot. Then add the water and the orange juice and stir. Now season with salt and pepper, bring to the boil and close the lid. Do not forget to stir. Let it simmer for about 10 - 12 minutes. After 6 minutes, add the frozen peas. Then turn off the heat, but continue to cook until the rice is ready. Season again and serve. Enjoy your meal.

Recipe 34: One-Pot "Asia-Pasta'"

Ingredients

- 1 onion
- 2 garlic cloves
- 1 courgette
- 1 pepper
- 80 g peas, frozen
- 250 g fusilli, pasta
- 2 tsp curry paste, red
- 250 ml coconut milk
- 250 g tomatoes, strained
- 1 tsp lemon juice
- 1 Salt
- 1 Pepper
- 1 tablespoon coconut oil
- 100 g cherry tomatoes

1. Peel and chop the onions and garlic. Then wash the peppers, remove the stalk, remove the seeds and cut into small pieces. Wash, peel and core the courgettes and cut into cubes. Also wash the cherry tomatoes and cut them in half. Now heat some oil in a pot. When the oil is hot, sauté the onions in it for about 2 - 3 minutes until translucent. Then add the garlic, courgettes and peppers and sauté for another 3 minutes. Then add the frozen peas and the fusilli noodles. Top up with the coconut milk. Now add the strained tomatoes, curry paste and lemon juice, mix well and bring to the boil. Simmer for approx. 10 -12 minutes, not forgetting to stir. Add the halved tomatoes 2 minutes before the end. The dish is ready when the pasta is al dente. Season with salt and pepper and serve. Enjoy it.

Recipe 35: One-Pot "Asian Noodles

Ingredients

- 1.5 tbsp. coconut oil
- 1 tbsp curry paste, red
- 1 tbsp soy sauce, alternatively tamari
- 3 spring onions
- 200 g tofu
- 400 ml coconut milk, reduced fat
- 600 ml vegetable stock
- 250 g rice noodles
- 200 g broccoli
- 1 pepper, red

1. First clean the spring onions and cut them into fine rings. Then wash again thoroughly and drain. Divide the broccoli into florets and wash them. Wash the peppers, remove the stalks, remove the seeds and cut into small pieces. Cut the tofu into cubes. Now heat the coconut oil in a pot. When the oil is hot, fry the curry paste in it. Then add the soy sauce, spring onions and tofu cubes. Sauté for approx. 3 - 5 minutes. Then pour in the coconut milk and vegetable stock and add the rice noodles, broccoli and peppers. Cover and simmer on a medium heat for about 5-8 minutes. When it is ready, season again and serve. Enjoy.

NOTES

Recipe 36: One-Pot Noodle Stew with Coconut Milk and Spinach

Ingredients

- 1 onion, organic
- 1 courgette, organic
- 1 tbsp. oil
- 140 g spinach, fresh or frozen
- 100 g peas, frozen
- 0.5 tsp vegetable stock, powder
- 300 g noodles
- 500 ml water, hot
- 250 ml coconut milk, reduced fat
- Lemon juice, from bottle
- 0.5 tsp turmeric
- Salt
- Curry powder
- 1 tsp ginger, freshly grated
- Pepper

1. Peel and chop the onions. Wash, halve and slice the courgettes. Wash and drain the spinach. You can put it aside for now. Heat some oil in a pot. When the oil is hot, sauté the onions for about 3 minutes on medium heat. Now add the courgette slices. Then add the spinach, the stock cubes, the chickpea pasta, the hot water, the coconut milk, the lemon juice and the turmeric. Bring everything to the boil. Now add the pasta, simmer over medium heat and don't forget to stir. The dish is ready when the pasta is al dente. Just before serving, bring to the boil again and season with salt and pepper. Add the spinach and serve. Enjoy your meal.

Recipe 37: One-Pot Chocolate Porridge

Now something sweet from the One-Pot.

Ingredients

- 70 g oat flakes
- 350 ml vegetable milk
- 150 ml water
- 1-2 tbsp raw cane sugar
- ½ tsp cardamom
- ½ tsp cinnamon
- 1 tablespoon cocoa

1. Put the oat flakes in a saucepan. Put the cooker on medium heat and add the oat flakes. Heat until the oat flakes begin to smell fragrant. Mix the water and the plant milk in a container and mix into the oat flakes. However, keep 50 ml as a remainder. Add the cocoa powder and mix with a whisk until there are no more lumps. Now add the cinnamon, cardamom and sugar. Bring the porridge to the boil, stirring constantly, and continue to simmer on medium heat for about 10 minutes until it has the desired consistency. Now stir in the cocoa milk and simmer for another 2 minutes. Do not forget to stir. Divide between 2 bowls, serve and enjoy.

NOTES

_____
_____

_____

_____

Recipe 38: One-Pot Pasta with Cashew Cheese Sauce

Ingredients

- 250 g noodles, gluten-free
- 1 large onion
- 250-500 ml vegetable stock
- 75 g cashew kernels
- 3 garlic cloves
- 100 g vegan cheese
- Salt
- Pepper
- 1 tablespoon lemon juice
- 3 tbsp. yeast flakes

1. Remove the pasta from the packet and cook according to the instructions. Meanwhile, peel and chop the onions and garlic. Bring 250 ml vegetable stock with the onions to the boil in a pan and then simmer for about 5 minutes. If the stock boils over during this time, you can add a little more. After the 5 minutes, add the garlic and more stock and simmer for another 5 minutes until the stock has evaporated completely. Put the onions, garlic and the rest of the ingredients into a blender and blend until homogeneous. Now taste and season if necessary. Then fold the mixture into the pasta with the vegan cheese. Mix well and serve.

NOTES

Recipe 39: One-Pot "Spaghetti Liguria

Ingredients

- 300 g spaghetti
- 250 g waxy potatoes
- 250 g green beans fresh
- 2 tsp salt
- 1 bunch basil
- 3 tbsp. yeast flakes
- 3 garlic cloves
- 2 tbsp cashew nuts
- 1 tbsp pine nuts
- 80 ml olive oil
- 1 tsp salt
- 1/2 tsp black pepper

1. Peel the potatoes and cut into slices about 1 cm thick. Wash the green beans, cut off the ends and cut into bite-sized pieces. Peel and chop the garlic. Cook the spaghetti according to the instructions on the packet. After about 3 minutes, add the potato slices to the boiling pasta water. One minute later, add the beans. To prepare the pesto, wash the basil and put the rest of the ingredients in a blender and blend well. When the pesto is thick, add a dash of the cooking water from the pasta until the desired consistency is reached. Drain the pasta and vegetables and return them to the pot dripping wet. Now stir in the pesto, season to taste and it is ready to serve.

Recipe 40: One-Pot "Spaghetti Catalogna

Ingredients

- 350 g wholemeal spaghetti
- a bunch of volcano asparagus
- 1 red onion
- 3 tbsp pine nuts
- 1 tbsp black sesame seeds
- 5 dried tomatoes, preserved in oil
- 1 chilli pepper
- 2 garlic cloves
- 5 tbsp olive oil
- Sea salt & freshly ground black pepper

1. Wash the volcano asparagus and cut into small pieces. Cut the large leaves crosswise into bite-sized pieces. Halve or quarter the shoots, depending on your preference. Peel and chop the garlic. Wash, seed and chop the chilli pepper. Cut the dried tomatoes into strips. Peel and chop the onions, preferably into strips. Now put the pasta into boiling salted water and simmer for about 8 minutes, according to the instructions on the packet. Meanwhile, make the sauce and roast the nuts. To do this, you need another pan and carefully toast the sesame seeds and the pine nuts. When the pine nuts are brown, remove from the heat. At the same time, heat 3 tablespoons of olive oil in another, larger pan and toss the garlic and onions in it. After about 1 minute, when the onions are translucent, add the volcano asparagus and sauté for a few minutes. Now turn the heat to medium and season with salt, pepper and the chilli pepper. Now skim off about 80 - 100 ml of the pasta water and add to the vegetables. Let the whole thing simmer for a while. The noodles can then be drained. Pour a little of the pasta water over the vegetables. Immediately add to the pasta. Mix in coarsely. Add the remaining olive oil and the roasted nuts. And it is ready to serve. Enjoy your meal.

Recipe 41: One-Pot "Spaghetti Porro"

Ingredients

- 1 large leek
- 2 carrots
- 3 cloves garlic
- 1 tsp salt (pasta water)
- 200 g spaghetti
- 3 tbsp. Teutoburg butter-flavoured rapeseed oil (alternatively: 3 tbsp. olive oil)
- 1 tsp thyme (dried)
- 1 tsp cayenne pepper
- 1 tsp black pepper
- 2 tsp salt
- 2-3 tbsp fresh parsley

1. To speed things up, make the pasta water in advance. In the meantime, wash the leek and cut it into pieces about 6 cm long, halve the sections and cut them into small strips. Peel the carrots and cut into small strips. Peel and chop the garlic. Salt the boiling pasta water and cook the spaghetti in it for about 8 minutes until it is al dente. In the meantime, put the olive oil, rapeseed oil and thyme in a hot pan, add the vegetables and sauté for about 3 - 4 minutes. Stir constantly. Add the garlic and sauté for about 1 minute. Season with salt and pepper. Take approx. 1 - 2 ladles of the pasta water and add it to the pan. Turn the heat down to the lowest setting and simmer gently until ready to serve. When the pasta is ready, drain. Gently turn the noodles in and place on the plate, then serve the vegetables directly on top. Finely chop the parsley and sprinkle over the top. Done.

Recipe 42: One-Pot "Spaghetti with Zucchini Ragout

Ingredients

- 250 g courgettes
- 1 onion
- 2 tbsp olive oil
- 1/2 tsp salt
- 250 g spaghetti
- 2 cloves garlic
- 125 ml soy milk or another unsweetened plant milk
- 4 tbsp. oat flakes
- 1 tbsp capers with broth
- 75 ml white wine
- 1 tsp oregano
- 3 tsp medium hot mustard

1. Wash and chop the courgettes. Peel and chop the onions and garlic. Now put some olive oil in a pan and heat it. When the oil is hot, add the onions and sauté over a medium heat for 3 minutes until translucent. Do not forget to stir. Then add the courgettes and season with salt. Sauté for another 3 minutes. Cook the spaghetti according to the instructions on the packet in plenty of salted water until al dente. Deglaze the vegetables with the white wine and then pour in the soy milk and add the oat flakes. Stir well, bring to the boil and simmer for about 5 minutes. Now add the garlic, mustard, oregano and capers to the sauce. Simmer over a low heat for about 2 minutes. Put the spaghetti on a plate, pour the sauce over it and it is ready to serve.

Recipe 43: One-Pot "Carrot Pasta with Green Asparagus and Hazelnuts

Ingredients

- 250-300 g wide ribbon noodles
- 200 g carrots
- 100 g green asparagus
- 2 sprigs thyme
- 1 tablespoon hazelnut oil
- 1-2 tbsp hazelnuts, chopped
- Salt

1. Wash and peel the carrots and cut them into thin strips. Also wash and peel the asparagus. Be careful of the woody part and cut or peel generously if necessary. Then cut into thin strips. Now take a pot and heat it with salted water. When the water is hot, add the tagliatelle and the thyme. Fill up with water until the noodles are covered and cook for about 10-15 minutes until the noodles are al dente. Add the carrot and asparagus strips about 5 minutes before. Once the pasta is ready and slightly cooked down, stir in the hazelnuts and hazelnut oil and then serve. Enjoy it.

NOTES

Recipe 44: One-Pot Ratatouille Paste with Olives

There and veggie: aubergines, courgettes and peppers with sun-drenched tomatoes and noodles in an aromatic stew - it really tastes like a holiday in the south!

Ingredients

- 1 medium aubergine
- 300 g courgettes
- 1 pepper, red
- 1 pepper, yellow
- 2 onions
- 2 garlic cloves
- 900 g ripe tomatoes (alternatively 1 can peeled tomatoes; 800 g)
- 4 tbsp olive oil
- Salt
- Pepper
- 2 tsp oregano, dried
- 300 g shell noodles
- 750 ml vegetable stock
- 100 g black olives with stone
- 4 stalks basil

1. Wash and clean the aubergine and courgette. Cut the peppers in half, remove the stalk, remove the seeds, wash the pods and cut them with the aubergine and courgette into approx. 1 cm cubes. Peel and chop the onions and garlic cloves. Wash the tomatoes, remove the stalks and cut the tomatoes into large pieces. Heat the olive oil in a pot. When the oil is hot, add the onions, garlic, aubergine, courgettes and peppers. Fry the whole thing over a medium heat for about 3 minutes. Stir well. Season the vegetables with salt, pepper and oregano. Now add the pasta and tomatoes and fill up with stock. Cover and bring to the boil over medium heat. Then let the pasta simmer uncovered over medium heat for about 15 minutes. Do not forget to stir. Add a little more water, depending on the consistency. Drain the olives and mix in. Wash and drain the basil. Pluck off the leaves and chop coarsely. Serve the ratatouille paste on plates and sprinkle with the basil.

Recipe 45: One-Pot Macaroni with Peas

Ingredients

- 1 bunch spring onions
- 250 g courgettes
- 2 garlic cloves
- 200 g frozen peas
- 4 tbsp olive oil
- 400 g short macaroni
- 1 l hot vegetable stock
- 150 g cheese, vegan
- Salt
- Pepper

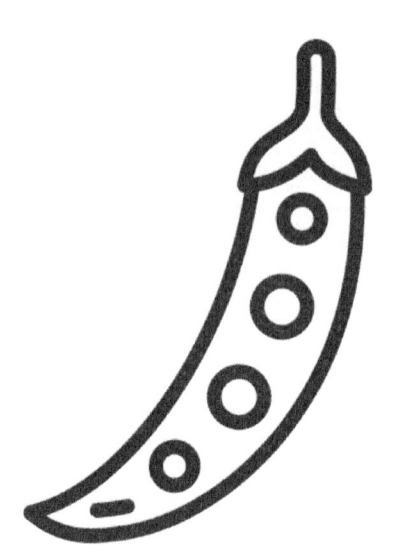

1. Wash and chop the spring onions. Wash the courgettes and cut into approx. 1 cm cubes. Peel and chop the garlic cloves. Allow the peas to thaw. Now heat some oil in a pot. When the oil is hot, sauté the spring onions over a medium heat until translucent. Then add the garlic, courgettes and pasta. Sauté for about 1 - 2 minutes. Then add the stock. Bring everything to the boil. Simmer on a medium heat for about 10 minutes without a lid. Do not forget to stir. Add the peas after about 5 minutes and stir in. In the meantime, grate the vegan cheese. When the pasta is al dente, mix two-thirds of the cheese into the pasta. Season everything with salt and pepper. After seasoning, serve on plates and sprinkle with cheese again. Enjoy your meal.

NOTES

Recipe 46: One-Pot Spaghetti with Asparagus Sugo

Ingredients

- 600 g green asparagus
- 1 Fennel
- 3 shallots
- 1 clove of garlic
- 2 tbsp pine nuts
- 4 tbsp olive oil
- 400 g spaghetti
- 2 cans peeled cherry tomatoes, chunky tomatoes as an alternative
- Salt
- Pepper
- 50 g hard cheese, vegan
- 4 stalks basil

1. Wash the asparagus. Remove the ends. Peel the stalks and look for the woody part. Cut the asparagus into pieces. Wash and clean the fennel, remove the stalk and cut into fine strips. Peel and chop the shallots and garlic. Roast the pine nuts in a pan without oil. When they are browned to your liking, take them out and leave them to cool on a plate. Now heat some oil in the pot. When the oil is hot, add the shallots, garlic and fennel and sauté everything over medium heat for about 2 - 3 minutes. Do not forget to stir. Add the spaghetti, the asparagus pieces, the cherry tomatoes and 2 tsp salt. Fill up with 750 ml of water. Bring to the boil with the lid on and then cook the pasta for about 10 - 12 minutes with the lid open and over a medium heat. Again, do not forget to stir. In the meantime, grate the cheese. Wash the basil, drain and pluck the leaves. Season the pasta with salt and pepper, serve on plates and sprinkle with cheese, pine nuts and basil.

Recipe 47: One-Pot Vegetable Noodles Once Hearty

Ingredients

- 2 carrots
- 3 Peppers, red
- 1 bunch spring onions
- 1 onion
- 1 clove of garlic
- Olive oil
- 1 teaspoon rose hot paprika powder
- 2 tbsp tomato paste
- 400 g noodles
- 500 ml vegetable stock
- ½ bunch parsley
- Salt
- Pepper

1. Wash, peel and chop the carrots. Wash the peppers, remove the stalk, remove the seeds and cut into small pieces. Wash the spring onions, cut into fine rings and wash again. Peel and chop the onions and garlic. Heat the olive oil in a pot. When the oil is hot, add the onions, garlic and carrots. Simmer over medium heat and stir well. Dust with paprika powder, then stir in the tomato paste and saute. Add the peppers and spring onions and sauté for about 2 minutes. Mix the noodles into the vegetables. Then add the stock. Make sure that everything is covered with liquid. Simmer on a low heat for about 5 minutes. Do not forget to stir. Meanwhile, wash and drain the parsley, pluck off the leaves and chop finely. Season to taste with salt and pepper, serve and sprinkle with parsley. Enjoy it.

Recipe 48: One-Pot Vegetable Pilaf with Nuts

Light, juicy and wonderfully uncomplicated: With colourful vegetables, turmeric, coriander and fruity-sweet extra, the Turkish rice stew seduces the senses.

- 4 small courgettes
- 2 carrots
- 2 red onions
- 2 garlic cloves
- 2 tbsp olive oil
- ½ tsp ground turmeric
- 1 tsp coriander seeds
- 250 g basmati rice
- 150 g nut mix with cranberries
- 600 ml vegetable stock
- 2 large tomatoes
- Salt | Pepper

1. Wash and slice the courgettes. Wash, peel and chop the carrots. Peel and chop the onions and garlic cloves. Now put some oil in a pot and heat it. When the oil is hot, add the onions, sprinkle with turmeric and sauté for about 2 minutes until translucent. Then add the coriander seeds and garlic and heat over medium heat for about 1 - 2 minutes until the spices are fragrant. Then stir in the rice and sauté until translucent. Add the nut mix, courgettes and carrots and sauté for about 2 minutes. Then pour in the stock and bring to the boil. Then simmer over medium heat for about 10 - 12 minutes. Do not forget to stir. Meanwhile, wash the tomatoes, remove the stalks, cut into quarters, remove the seeds and cut into small cubes. Now fold the tomatoes into the rice and cook, covered, over a low heat for about 10 minutes. Season with salt and pepper, serve and enjoy. Enjoy.

Recipe 49: One-Pot Quinoa - Bowl with Sweet Potatoes

Ingredients

- 1 sweet potato (approx. 300 g)
- 300 g green beans, frozen
- 1 can corn
- 2 tomatoes
- 250 g quinoa
- 500 ml vegetable stock
- 1 tablespoon tomato paste
- 1 tsp ground cumin
- 2 tbsp jalapeño chillies, chopped
- 1 ripe avocado
- 2 tbsp lime juice
- ½ pomegranate
- Salt
- Pepper

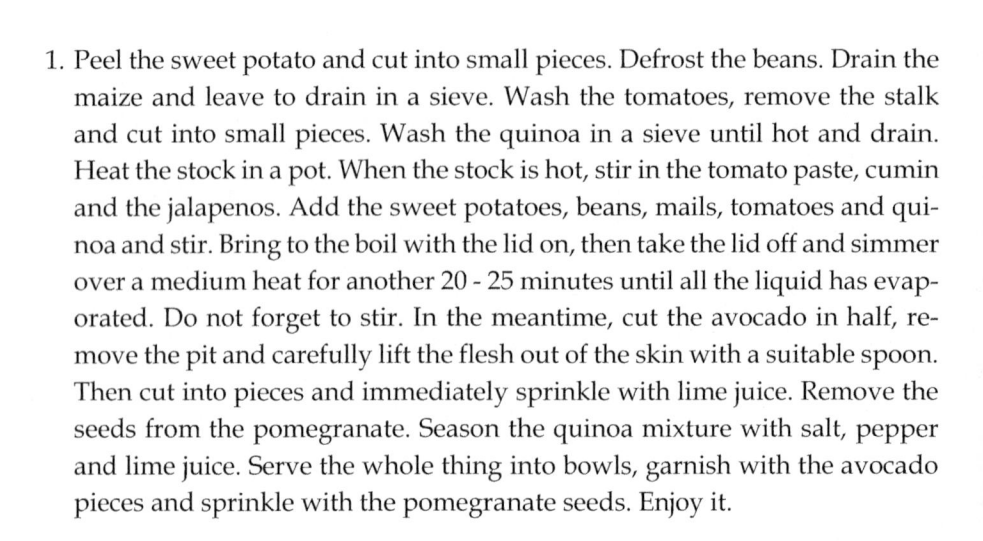

1. Peel the sweet potato and cut into small pieces. Defrost the beans. Drain the maize and leave to drain in a sieve. Wash the tomatoes, remove the stalk and cut into small pieces. Wash the quinoa in a sieve until hot and drain. Heat the stock in a pot. When the stock is hot, stir in the tomato paste, cumin and the jalapenos. Add the sweet potatoes, beans, mails, tomatoes and quinoa and stir. Bring to the boil with the lid on, then take the lid off and simmer over a medium heat for another 20 - 25 minutes until all the liquid has evaporated. Do not forget to stir. In the meantime, cut the avocado in half, remove the pit and carefully lift the flesh out of the skin with a suitable spoon. Then cut into pieces and immediately sprinkle with lime juice. Remove the seeds from the pomegranate. Season the quinoa mixture with salt, pepper and lime juice. Serve the whole thing into bowls, garnish with the avocado pieces and sprinkle with the pomegranate seeds. Enjoy it.

Recipe 50: One-Pot Curry, Spinach - Millet with Mushrooms

Ingredients

- 500 g mixed mushrooms
- 1 onion
- 2 garlic cloves
- 2 tbsp. oil
- 2 tbsp. soy sauce
- Olive oil
- 250 g millet
- 2 tsp curry powder
- Salt
- 1 l vegetable stock
- 200 g baby spinach
- 2 tsp lemon juice
- Pepper

1. Clean the mushrooms, preferably with kitchen paper. Remove the stalk and then cut the mushrooms into coarse pieces. Peel and chop the onions and garlic. Now heat some oil in a pot. When the oil is hot, add the mushrooms and fry over a medium heat for about 5 minutes. Stir well until they are light brown. Transfer the mushrooms to a bowl, season with soy sauce and set aside, still covered. Heat the olive oil in a saucepan. When the oil is hot, sauté the onions and garlic in it, over medium heat for about 2 - 3 minutes. Then add the millet and sauté for about 1 minute. Add the curry and sauté briefly. Season to taste with salt and pepper, add the stock and bring to the boil. Then cook without a lid for about 20 - 25 minutes, stirring occasionally. In the meantime, wash and trim the spinach. At the end of the cooking time, place the spinach on top of the millet, cover and let it collapse for another 2 - 3 minutes. Then fold in the spinach and season again with salt and pepper and lemon juice. Arrange everything on plates, top with the fried mushrooms and enjoy.

Recipe 51: One-Pot Hot Taboule with Halloumi

Ingredients

- 2 Pack. Halloumi, vegan
- 1 cucumber
- 4 tomatoes
- 4 spring onions
- 5 tbsp olive oil
- 300 g bulgur
- 2 tsp tomato paste
- 600 ml vegetable stock
- 1 bunch parsley
- Salt
- 3 tbsp. lemon juice
- 1 tsp Pul Biber (hot pepper flakes)

1. Pat the halloumi dry, preferably with kitchen paper, and cut into slices about 1 cm thick. Wash and peel the cucumber and cut into short, thin strips. Wash the tomatoes, remove the stalk and cut into small pieces. Wash the spring onions, cut into fine rings and wash again. Heat the oil in a pot. When the oil is hot, fry the halloumi in batches until both sides are golden brown. Then remove and set aside, covered. Briefly sauté the bulgur and tomato paste in the frying fat. Pour in the stock and bring to the boil. Cover and leave to swell over a medium heat for about 10 minutes. In the meantime, wash and drain the parsley and chop the leaves finely. Now loosen the bulgur with a fork, season with salt, lemon juice and pul beaver. Fold the tomatoes, cucumber, spring onions, some parsley and the olive oil into the bulgur. Place the fried halloumi slices on top of the bulgur, cover and cook for another 5 minutes on a low heat. Arrange the whole thing on plates, sprinkle with the rest of the parsley and serve.

Recipe 52: One-Pot Potato - Broccoli

It doesn't get any juicier than this! Vegetables in an aromatic lemon and cheese cream sauce, topped with fine fish: the Schlemmertopf is also a great Sunday dinner.

Ingredients

- 800 g mainly waxy potatoes
- 3 carrots
- 400 g broccoli
- 1 onion
- 1 organic lemon
- 2 tbsp. oil
- 150 ml vegetable stock
- 250 g vegetable cream
- 30 g Gouda, vegan
- Salt
- Pepper
- ½ bunch dill

1. Peel and wash the potatoes and cut into approx. 1 cm cubes. Clean and peel the carrots, then cut them into thin slices. Wash and clean the broccoli and cut into small florets. Peel the stems and cut into small cubes. Peel and chop the onions. Wash the lemon in hot water, dry it and grate about 1 tsp of zest. Heat the oil in a pot. When the oil is hot, add the onions and sauté for about 5 minutes over medium heat. Add the potatoes, carrots and broccoli. Mix everything well. Then pour in the vegetable cream and stock. Bring everything to the boil and simmer over a medium heat, stirring occasionally, until creamy. Meanwhile, wash and chop the dill. Grate the cheese. Season with salt, pepper and the lemon zest, serve and sprinkle the dill and cheese on top. Enjoy your meal.

Recipe 53: One-Pot Potato - Pumpkin

Paprika-spicy, lemon-fresh and wonderfully creamy: the veggie ragout of pumpkin, potatoes and tomatoes is a convincingly light and colourful meal.

Ingredients

- 1 kg butternut squash, alternatively Hokkaido squash
- 500 g waxy potatoes
- 4 carrots
- 2 peppers, red
- 2 onions
- 2 garlic cloves
- 5 tbsp. oil
- Salt | Pepper
- 2 teaspoons sweet paprika powder
- 1 teaspoon rose hot paprika powder
- 1 tablespoon tomato paste
- 500 ml vegetable stock
- 200 g strained tomatoes (tin)

1. Clean and peel the pumpkin. Carefully remove the fibres and seeds with a suitable spoon. Wash and peel the potatoes and carrots. Cut everything together to about the same size. Wash the peppers, remove the stalk, remove the seeds and cut into small pieces. Peel and chop the onions and garlic. Heat the oil in a pot. When the oil is hot, sauté the onions in it over medium heat for about 2 minutes. Add the pumpkin, potatoes, carrots, peppers and garlic and sauté over medium heat for about 2 - 3 minutes. Season everything together with salt, pepper and both types of pepper. Stir in the tomato paste and sauté for 2 - 3 minutes. Add the stock and tomatoes. Don't forget to stir and let it simmer on a medium heat for about 25 minutes. At the end, season again with salt and pepper and serve in deep plates. Enjoy your meal.

Recipe 54: One-Pot Chanterelle - Gnocchi - Ragout

Ingredients

- 250 g chanterelles
- 250 g mushrooms
- 3 shallots
- 2 garlic cloves
- 2 tbsp olive oil
- 75 ml dry sherry, alternatively vegetable stock
- 500 g gnocchi
- 100 ml vegetable stock
- 200 g vegetable cream
- 1 tsp dried thyme
- 150 g cherry tomatoes
- ½ bunch parsley
- Salt
- Pepper

1. Clean the mushrooms, preferably with kitchen paper. Small chanterelles can be left whole, all others cut into coarse pieces. Peel and chop the shallots and garlic. Heat the oil in a pot. When the oil is hot, sauté the shallots and garlic in it over medium heat until translucent. Then add the mushrooms and sauté for 2 - 3 minutes. Stir well. Deglaze with the sherry or vegetable stock and add the thyme. Bring everything to the boil and then simmer over medium heat for about 10 minutes. Again, do not forget to stir. Meanwhile, wash and halve the cherry tomatoes. Wash and drain the parsley, pluck the leaves and chop them. Season the mushroom ragout with salt and pepper. Then mix in the tomatoes and parsley and bring to the boil again briefly. Now serve the whole thing in deep plates and add a few flakes of parsley and enjoy.

Recipe 55: One-Pot Potato - Chard - Vegetables

Ingredients

- 500 g chard
- 600 g mainly waxy potatoes
- 2 peppers, red
- 1 onion
- 1 clove of garlic
- 2 tbsp olive oil
- Salt
- Pepper
- 400 g tomatoes, canned, chunky
- 1 ½ tbsp tomato paste
- 2 tsp balsamic vinegar
- 50 g hard cheese, vegan

1. Wash the chard, cut the stems into small cubes and the leaves into strips about 1 cm wide. Peel the potatoes and cut into cubes. Wash the peppers, remove the stalk, remove the seeds and cut into small pieces. Peel and chop the onions and garlic. Heat the oil in a pot. When the oil is hot, sauté the onions and garlic until translucent. Add the chard stems, potatoes and peppers and sauté over a medium heat for 2 - 3 minutes. Stir well. Season with salt and pepper. Add the tomatoes, tomato paste, balsamic vinegar and 300 ml water. Bring everything to the boil. Cook without a lid over medium heat for approx. 10 - 12 minutes until the sauce is nice and creamy. Do not forget to stir. Now, put the chopped chard leaves on top and let it simmer with the lid on for another 5 minutes. Stir once, season again with salt and pepper and serve. Sprinkle the grated vegan hard cheese on top and enjoy.

Recipe 56: One-Pot Potato - Lentils

Ingredients

- 1 onion
- 2 garlic cloves
- 1 tbsp. oil
- 150 g plate lentils
- 1.2 l vegetable stock
- 1 tsp dried marjoram
- 500 g waxy potatoes
- 1 leek
- 2 carrots
- Salt
- Pepper
- ½ bunch chives

1. Peel and chop the onions and garlic. Heat the oil in a pot. When the oil is hot, sauté the onions and garlic until translucent. Then add the lentils and sauté for about 1 - 2 minutes. Then fill up with stock and add the marjoram. Cover and bring to the boil, then simmer on a low heat for about 30 minutes. Meanwhile, peel the potatoes and cut into cubes. Wash the leeks, cut them into rings and wash and drain them again. Peel and halve the carrots lengthwise and then cut into slices. About 10 minutes before the end of the cooking time, add the potatoes, carrots and leeks to the lentils, bring to the boil again and simmer, covered. In the meantime, wash, drain and chop the chives. Season the stew with salt and pepper, serve and garnish the deep plates with chives. Enjoy it.

Recipe 57: One-Pot "Winter" with Chestnuts

The Italian classic surprises here with Brussels sprouts, chestnuts and white beans as a filling feel-good stew - a real sunshine dish for cold days.

Ingredients

- 2 onions
- 2 garlic cloves
- 400 g Brussels sprouts
- 2 carrots
- 3 tbsp olive oil
- 1 can tomatoes, 400 g, chunky
- 2 tsp dried oregano
- 600 ml vegetable stock
- Salt
- Pepper
- 200 g cooked chestnuts
- 1 can white beans
- ½ bunch parsley
- 50 g vegan hard cheese

1. Peel and chop the onions and garlic. Wash and clean the Brussels sprouts. Depending on the size, the Brussels sprouts may be halved. Peel and slice the carrots. Heat the oil in a pot. When the oil is hot, add the onions, garlic, Brussels sprouts and carrots and sauté over medium heat for about 2 - 3 minutes. Then add the tomatoes, oregano and the stock. Season everything together with salt and pepper and bring to the boil once. Then simmer over medium heat for approx. 10 - 15 minutes. In the meantime, remove the chestnuts from the package and cut them into pieces as desired. Drain the white beans, wash and drain in a sieve. Add both ingredients to the stew about 5 minutes before the end of the cooking time and cook over a low heat. Meanwhile, wash and drain the parsley, pluck off the leaves and chop. Grate the cheese. Season the stew again and serve in deep plates, sprinkle with the parsley and cheese and enjoy.

Recipe 58: One-Pot Tajine, Vegetables and Chickpeas

Aromatic pleasure: The hearty ragout from North Africa is gently braised with potatoes, romanesco and Ras el Hanout, an oriental spice blend.

Ingredients

- 500 g mainly waxy potatoes
- 500 g romanesco, alternatively cauliflower
- 200 g shallots
- 4 garlic cloves
- 4 tbsp olive oil
- 2 ½ tsp Ras el Hanout (oriental spice mixture)
- Salt | Pepper
- 400 ml vegetable stock
- 1 tin of chickpeas (250 g drained weight)
- 250 g cherry tomatoes
- 150 g vegan cream yoghurt
- 1 tsp cornflour
- 6 stalks parsley

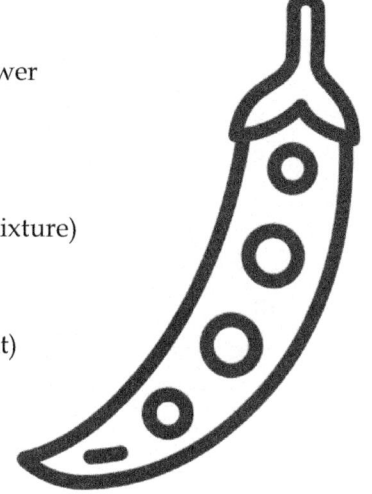

1. Peel the potatoes and cut them into large pieces. Wash the romanesco and cut into small florets. Peel and chop the shallots and garlic. Heat the oil in a pot. When the oil is hot, add the shallots and sauté over medium heat, stirring, for about 3 minutes. Add the potatoes, romansco and garlic. Sauté everything over a low heat for about 2 - 3 minutes. Sprinkle Ras El Hanout over the top and season the whole mixture with salt and pepper. Now make the stock and pour over it. Cover, bring to the boil and simmer over a medium heat for about 20 minutes. In the meantime, drain the chickpeas in a sieve. Wash and halve the cherry tomatoes. Mix the vegan yoghurt with the cornflour and add to the vegetables and simmer for 2 - 3 minutes. When the sauce has thickened, stir in the chickpeas and tomatoes and leave to heat through. It takes about 2 - 3 minutes. Season everything again with salt and pepper, possibly also with a little Ras El Hanout, then pour into deep plates and sprinkle with parsley. Ready to enjoy.

Recipe 59: One-Pot Bean - Paprika

Ingredients

- 1 pepper, red
- 1 pepper, yellow
- 1 onion
- 1 clove of garlic
- 1 tablespoon olive oil
- ½ tbsp. sweet paprika powder
- 1 tsp dried oregano
- 1 l vegetable stock
- 100 g small shell noodles
- 1 tin of white beans (e.g. giant white beans; 250 g drained weight)
- 100 g green olives (stuffed with paprika)
- ½ bunch parsley
- Salt
- Pepper

1. Wash the peppers, remove the stalk, remove the seeds and cut into small pieces. Peel and chop the onions and garlic. Heat the oil in a pot. When the oil is hot, sauté the onions and garlic at medium temperature for about 2 minutes. Do not forget to stir. Then sauté the pepper pieces, season with oregano and deglaze with the stock. Then bring to the boil once, cover and cook over a medium heat for about 5 minutes. Then add the pasta, bring to the boil and let everything simmer together. Simmer until the pasta is al dente. In the meantime, wash the beans and drain in a sieve. Drain the olives in the same way. Add both to the stew about 2 minutes before the end of the cooking time. Wash and drain the parsley, pluck the leaves and chop them. Season to taste with salt and pepper and serve, sprinkling with parsley and enjoying.

Recipe 60: One-Pot Green Bulgur with Beans

Ingredients

- 250 g frozen broad beans
- 300 g green beans
- 1 kohlrabi
- 1 onion
- 2 garlic cloves
- 2 tbsp olive oil
- 600 ml vegetable stock
- Salt
- Pepper
- 100 g frozen peas
- 200 g bulgur
- 1 bunch of mixed herbs (e.g. basil, tarragon, parsley, chives)
- 1 organic lemon

1. Defrost the broad beans in a bowl of warm water, then squeeze the seeds out of the beans. Wash the green beans and cut them into bite-sized pieces. Wash the kohlrabi. Put the tender leaves to one side. Then peel the kohlrabi and cut into pieces. Peel and chop the onions and garlic. Heat the oil in a pot. When the oil is hot, add the onion and sauté over a medium heat until translucent. Then add the green beans, the frozen bean seeds, the kohlrabi and the garlic and sauté for about 1 - 2 minutes. Then add the vegetable stock. Season to taste with salt and pepper, then bring to the boil and cook without a lid for about 10 minutes over a medium heat. Do not forget to stir. Then add the peas and bulgur, bring to the boil again and simmer over a low heat with the lid on for about 10 minutes. In the meantime, wash and drain the kohlrabi leaves and herbs. Then pluck the herbs and chop them together with the kohlrabi leaves. Wash the lemon in hot water and dry it. Finely grate 1 tsp of the zest and squeeze out the juice. Season the stew again and add the lemon zest and juice. Then fold in the herb and kohlrabi leaf mixture and serve.

Recipe 61: One-Pot Fresh Vegetable Rice Pan

Ingredients

- 150 g rice
- 1 medium aubergine
- ½ small courgette
- 50 g green peas
- 1 small carrot
- 60 g broccoli
- 25 g mushrooms, thinly sliced
- ½ small red onion, chopped
- 75 ml water
- 1 pinch paprika seasoning
- 1 pinch ginger spice
- ½ small clove of garlic, minced
- 20 ml soy/teriyaki sauce
- 1 pinch sugar
- 2 tbsp sesame/canola oil
- Salt and pepper

1. Wash the aubergine and cut into strips approx. 2.5 cm wide. Wash the courgette and cut into small pieces. Peel the carrot and cut into small pieces. Heat a pot with 250 ml water. When the water is hot, add the carrot and onions. Simmer for about 5 minutes with the lid closed. Then remove the lid and stir in the rest of the vegetables and the oil. Continue to simmer over a medium heat for approx. 5 - 7 minutes. Then add the spices, followed by the rice and stir everything together evenly. Add more water if necessary. Once the rice is cooked, remove the pan from the heat and leave to stand for another 15-20 minutes. Then serve and enjoy.

Recipe 62: One-Pot Colourful Spinach Rice

Ingredients

- 350 g fresh spinach leaves
- 100 g rice
- ½ onion
- ½ carrot
- ½ Paprika
- 2 ½ tbsp olive oil
- 200 ml water

1. Wash and drain the spinach. Peel and chop the onion and carrot. Wash the pepper, remove the stalk, remove the seeds and cut into small pieces. Heat the oil in a pan. When the oil is hot, add the onion and carrot and cook, stirring occasionally, until everything is soft. Then add the rice and pepper. Do not forget to stir. Now add the 200 ml of water. Stir constantly to increase the consistency as the rice absorbs the water. Let it cook for about 10 minutes. Season with salt and pepper if necessary. In the meantime, cut the spinach into strips and add to the rice. Let everything cook together until the spinach is limp. Then remove the pan from the heat and serve. Enjoy your meal.

NOTES

Recipe 63: One-Pot Carrot - Onion - Risotto

Ingredients

- 150 g rice
- 150 g cauliflower
- 2 carrots
- 20 g tofu
- ½ medium onion
- 60 g broccoli
- ½ tsp garlic paste
- 1 ½ small tomatoes
- 200 ml vegetable stock
- 1 tablespoon olive oil
- Salt
- Pepper

1. First, cut the tofu into small cubes. Peel the carrots and cut into small pieces. Peel and chop the onion. Wash the cauliflower and separate into florets. Also wash the broccoli and separate into florets. Wash and chop the tomatoes. Heat the oil in a pot. Add the vegetable stock. Stir in the cauliflower, rice, broccoli, tofu, garlic paste, onion, tomatoes and carrots. Simmer for about 45 minutes, stirring occasionally. When the rice is cooked, season briefly with salt and pepper and serve. Enjoy it.

NOTES

Recipe 64: One-Pot Mushroom Risotto

Ingredients

- ½ tsp olive oil
- 1 onion
- 2 garlic cloves
- 150 g rice
- 1 bay leaf
- 75g mushrooms
- 1 tsp mushrooms chopped in a blender
- 300 ml vegetable stock
- 2 shallots
- Parsley, chopped, to taste
- 1 tsp balsamic vinegar
- Salt
- Pepper

1. Peel and chop the onions, shallots and garlic. Wash and pluck the parsley. Cut the plucked leaves into small pieces. Clean the mushrooms and chop them in a blender. Heat the oil in a pot. When the oil is hot, fry the onions, stirring all the time. Add the garlic and the rice. Add the bay leaf, the chopped mushrooms and the mushroom paste. Bring to the boil for 2 minutes and add the vegetable stock. Put the lid on and cook at a high temperature for about 3 - 5 minutes. Then remove the lid and add the shallots and vinegar. Depending on the desired consistency, add a little more water or continue to simmer. Season to taste and serve. Enjoy.

Recipe 65: One-Pot Breakfast Quinoa, Sweet

Ingredients

- 225 g quinoa
- 250 ml water
- 1 teaspoon maple syrup
- ¼ tsp vanilla
- 1 pinch cinnamon
- 1 pinch of salt
- 25 g blueberries
- 25 g almonds
- Vegetable milk to taste

1. Wash the quinoa thoroughly and drain. Place in a saucepan with the water, syrup, vanilla, cinnamon and salt and cook on the highest heat for approx. 2 minutes without a lid. Then put the lid on and simmer for another 10 - 15 minutes at medium temperature. Do not forget to stir. Make sure that the quinoa has risen. Pour into bowls and serve with blueberries, almonds and/or vegetable milk.

NOTES

Recipe 66: One-Pot White Beans and Vegetables on Pasta

Ingredients

- 560 g creamed spinach
- 500 ml water
- 150 g macaroni
- 60 ml vegetable stock
- 1 tablespoon olive oil
- ½ small clove of garlic
- 220g white beans
- Salt
- Pepper

1. Heat the water in a pot, add salt and wait until it boils. Add the macaroni to the water and cook until al dente. It takes about 10 - 12 minutes. Meanwhile, peel and chop the garlic and mix with the olive oil. Now add the white beans and the vegetable stock. Simmer for 2 minutes until the beans are cooked. Remove the pan from the heat and mix the spinach into the pasta. Now season with salt and pepper and serve. Enjoy your meal.

NOTES

_____
_____

Recipe 67: One-Pot Black Bean Burrito

Ingredients

- 1 tsp coconut oil
- ½ paprika, red crushed
- ½ pepper, chopped green
- ½ small onion, minced
- 130 g black beans
- 120 g tofu, diced
- 80 g long grain rice
- 60 ml salsa
- 130 g corn
- 25 g peas
- 1 heaped tablespoon coriander
- 120 g dried tomatoes
- 175 ml vegetable stock
- 1 tbsp paprika seasoning
- 1 tbsp garlic seasoning
- 1 tbsp cumin
- 1 tsp onion spice
- 120 g grated vegan hard cheese
- 2 large tortilla wraps
- Salt
- Pepper

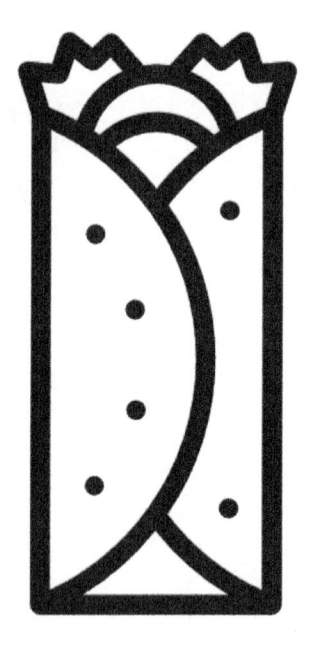

1. Wash the peppers, red and green, remove the stalk, remove the seeds and cut into small pieces. Drain the tofu and then dice. Heat the coconut oil in a pot over medium heat. When the oil is hot, fry the onions, peppers and tofu for about 5 minutes. Then add the vegetable stock and the rest of the ingredients, except for the spices. Simmer everything together for about 20 minutes. Now remove from the heat and stir in the spices. Prepare tortilla wraps and fill with the contents of the pot, sprinkle with some grated vegan hard cheese and eat. Enjoy.

Recipe 68: One-Pot Sweet Potato - Coconut - Curry

Ingredients

- ½ tsp coconut oil
- 100 g onion
- 100 g dried red lentils
- 1 medium sweet potato
- 1 large carrot
- ½ tsp turmeric spice
- 1 tbsp mild curry powder
- 1 tsp ginger spice
- 500 ml vegetable stock
- 175 ml coconut milk
- Salt
- Pepper

1. Peel and chop the onion. Peel and dice the sweet potato. Peel the carrot and cut into small strips. Heat the coconut oil in a pot. When the oil is hot, fry the onions until they are lightly golden. Then add the lentils, sweet potatoes, carrot and spices. Mix everything well. Then add the vegetable stock and bring to the boil. Simmer at a low temperature for about 25 minutes. As soon as the sweet potato is soft, stir in the coconut milk. Then season with salt and pepper and it is ready to serve.

NOTES

Recipe 69: One-Pot Lentils in Tomato Sauce

Ingredients

- ½ small onion, minced
- 50 g tomatoes, chopped
- 50 g lentils
- 185 ml water
- 1 stick of celery, chopped whole with stalk and leaves
- 1 pepper, green
- 1 tablespoon olive oil
- 1 tsp curry powder (as required)
- Salt
- Pepper

1. Peel and chop the onion. Wash the tomatoes, remove the stalk and cut into small pieces. Wash the peppers, remove the stalk, remove the seeds and cut into small pieces. Heat the olive oil in a pot. When the oil is hot, fry the onions, celery and peppers in it until the onion softens. Then add the tomatoes and the spices. Then add the water and the lentils, mixing everything well. Now bring the whole thing to the boil and simmer with the lid closed, at a medium temperature, for about 15 minutes. The lentils should no longer be soft. Season to taste and serve. Enjoy your meal.

NOTES

_____

_____

Recipe 70: One-Pot Couscous Salad

Ingredients

- 115 g couscous
- 2 spring onions
- 1 pepper, red
- 250 g corn
- 2 tbsp olive oil
- 2 potatoes
- 850 ml water
- Parsley, chopped as required
- Brown sugar, as required
- Lemon juice, as required
- Soy sauce, as required
- Salt
- Pepper

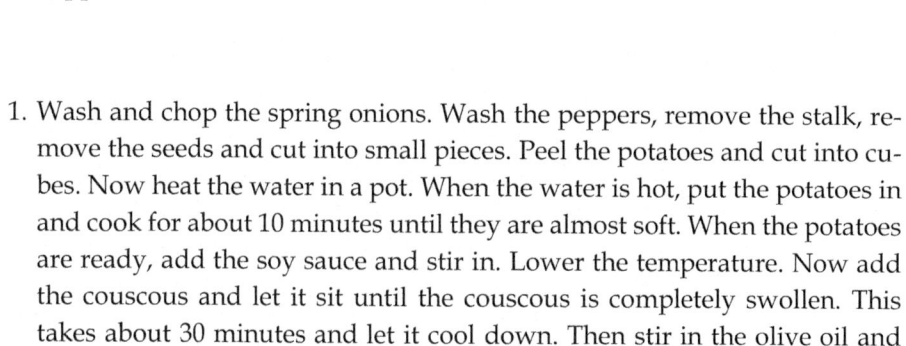

1. Wash and chop the spring onions. Wash the peppers, remove the stalk, remove the seeds and cut into small pieces. Peel the potatoes and cut into cubes. Now heat the water in a pot. When the water is hot, put the potatoes in and cook for about 10 minutes until they are almost soft. When the potatoes are ready, add the soy sauce and stir in. Lower the temperature. Now add the couscous and let it sit until the couscous is completely swollen. This takes about 30 minutes and let it cool down. Then stir in the olive oil and brown sugar. Use this to make a vinaigrette. Then add the remaining spices and season to taste, ready. Enjoy it.

Recipe 71: One-Pot Mexican Quinoa

Ingredients

- 1 tablespoon olive oil
- ½ onion
- 1 clove of garlic
- ½ paprika, red
- ½ paprika, yellow
- Cumin
- Paprika seasoning
- Chilli powder
- 150 g quinoa
- ½ medium sweet potato
- 120 g tomatoes
- Mild chillies
- 120 g black beans
- 125 ml vegetable stock
- Juice of a large lime
- 20g fresh coriander, chopped
- Salt
- Pepper

1. Peel and chop the onions and garlic clove. Wash the peppers, remove the stalk, remove the seeds and cut into small pieces. Wash and peel the sweet potato and cut into small cubes. Wash the tomatoes and cut into small pieces. Also wash the chillies, remove the stalk, remove the seeds and cut into small pieces. Now heat the olive oil in a pot. When the oil is hot, fry the onions and garlic for about 5 minutes. Now add the sweet potatoes and cook, adding a little water until the potato pieces are covered. After about 4 minutes, add the peppers and spices and season to taste. Then let it cook for about 3 - 5 minutes. Then top up with the vegetable stock and bring to the boil again. When it boils, add the quinoa, tomatoes and beans and stir well. Let the whole thing simmer for about 20 minutes with the lid closed. As soon as the quinoa has fully absorbed the liquid and is thus also swollen, remove the pot from the cooker, season again with the spices and add the lime juice. It is ready to serve.

Recipe 72: One-Pot Tomato and Herb Soup

Ingredients

- 225 g tomatoes
- 175 ml vegetable stock
- 2-3 basil leaves, chopped
- 1 clove of garlic
- 1 onion
- 1 carrot
- Paprika seasoning, to taste
- 1 tablespoon olive oil
- 50 g grated vegan hard cheese
- Salt
- Pepper

1. Wash the tomatoes, remove the stalk and cut into small pieces. Peel and chop the onion and garlic. Peel the carrots and cut them into small pieces. Bring the vegetable stock to the boil in a pot. When the stock is hot, add all the ingredients, except for the hard cheese, and simmer at a low temperature for about 2 hours. When the vegetables are soft, remove the pot from the heat and allow to cool completely. Then skim off about a third of the soup and blend separately. Blend until a creamy, thick consistency is reached. Return this to the soup pot and stir into the soup until everything is evenly distributed. Bring the whole thing to the boil again for about 2 minutes, pour into a deep dish, sprinkle the hard cheese on top and the soup is ready.

NOTES

_____
_____

Recipe 73: One-Pot Tomato and Pepper Soup

Ingredients

- ½ onion
- 1 clove of garlic
- 2 peppers, red
- 2 tomatoes
- 500 ml vegetable stock
- 2 tablespoons virgin olive oil
- 1 bay leaf

1. Peel and chop the onion and garlic clove. Wash the tomatoes, remove the stalk and cut into small pieces. Wash the peppers, remove the stalk, remove the seeds and cut into small pieces. Now heat the olive oil in a pot. When the oil is hot, add the onions and garlic and fry for about 3 - 4 minutes. Then add the peppers, tomatoes and bay leaf. Let it simmer for about 10 minutes on a low heat. Add a little water if necessary. After 10 minutes, add the stock and season with salt and pepper. Now bring the whole thing to the boil and simmer on a low heat for about 20 minutes. Then remove the bay leaf and serve. Enjoy

NOTES

Recipe 74: One-Pot Creamy Potato Soup

Ingredients

- 2-3 potatoes
- ½ carrot
- ¼ courgette
- ¼ celery bunch
- 600 ml water
- 1 tablespoon olive oil
- Some dried rosemary
- Salt
- Pepper
- Some fresh parsley, finely chopped

1. Peel the potatoes and cut into small cubes. Peel and chop the carrot. Wash and chop the courgettes. Also wash and chop the celery. Heat the olive oil in a pot. When the oil is hot, fry the vegetables and the rosemary in it. Now take half of the water and add it to the pot. Now bring the whole thing to the boil. Then continue to simmer over a low heat until the vegetables are nice and tender. Then blend everything well with a hand blender and season to taste. Now it is time to serve. Garnish the soup with a touch of pepper and sprinkle some parsley on top. Enjoy your meal.

NOTES

Recipe 75: One-Pot Pea, Dill and Rice Soup

Ingredients

- ½ pack peas, frozen
- ½ onion
- 2 garlic cloves
- 75 g rice
- 500 ml vegetable stock
- 1.5 tbsp fresh dill, chopped
- 1.5 tbsp virgin olive oil
- Salt
- Pepper

1. Peel and chop the onions and garlic. Heat the olive oil in a pot. When the oil is hot, fry the onions and garlic for about 3 - 4 minutes. Stir several times. Now add the stock and then the peas. Bring everything to the boil. Then stir in the rice, cover the pot with a lid and set the heat to medium. Let it simmer for about 15 minutes. Then add the dill, season to taste and serve. Decorate with some dill. Done.

NOTES

Recipe 76: One-Pot Vegan Breakfast Cereal

Ingredients

- 125 g oat flakes
- 1 peach, pitted, crushed
- 125 ml coconut milk
- 1 vanilla pod, scraped out
- Maple syrup, to taste
- 20 g chopped almonds
- 1 tablespoon coconut oil

1. Wash, stone and chop the peach. Put the oat flakes in a pot and toast gently. If necessary, you can add a tablespoon of coconut oil. When the flakes are toasted, add the coconut milk. Wait briefly until everything has come to the boil and then add the peaches and vanilla. Close the lid and simmer for about 3 - 5 minutes. Serve while still warm with almonds and/or maple syrup. Enjoy it.

NOTES

Recipe 77: One-Pot Gnocchi with Chickpeas

Ingredients

- 120 g gnocchi
- 2 tbsp olive oil
- 2 cloves of garlic, crushed
- Dried oregano, to taste
- Dried basil, to taste
- 150 g mushrooms, sliced
- 50 g broccoli
- 250 g chickpeas
- 250 ml water
- Salt
- Pepper

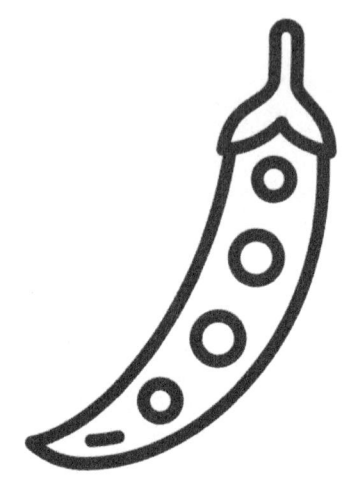

1. Clean the mushrooms, preferably with kitchen paper, and then slice them. Peel and chop the garlic. Put the water in a pan and bring to the boil with a pinch of salt. Then cook the gnocchi for a maximum of 5 minutes until they are firm to the bite. Then drain the water and set the pasta aside. Heat the olive oil in the same pan and fry the garlic briefly. Then add the gnocchi and sauté for another 2 - 4 minutes. Then add the rest of the ingredients and about 50 ml of water. Now simmer again for about 10 - 15 minutes. Do not forget to stir. Now season to taste and serve.

NOTES

_____

_____

Recipe 78: One-Pot Mushrooms in Cream

Ingredients

- 1 onion, chopped
- 15 g olive oil
- 175 g mushrooms
- Freshly grated nutmeg
- 200 ml vegetable cream
- Paprika seasoning, to taste
- Salt
- Pepper

1. Peel and chop the onions. Clean the mushrooms, preferably with kitchen paper, and cut them into small pieces. Heat the olive oil in a pot. When the oil is hot, add the onions and sauté for about 2 minutes until translucent. Then sauté the mushrooms for about 2 minutes. Then add the vegetable cream and bring to the boil. Cover the lid and simmer for about 10 minutes. Then season with the spices and serve with a piece of bread. Enjoy it.

NOTES

_____
_____
_____
_____

Recipe 79: One-Pot Tomato - Coconut Noodles

Ingredients

- 30 g unroasted coconut chips
- 1 pepper, red
- 2 shallots
- 2 garlic cloves
- 20 g ginger
- 100 g frozen peas
- 200 ml creamy coconut milk
- 200 ml tomatoes (tin), chunky
- Salt
- 150 g baby spinach
- 2 - 3 tbsp lime juice

1. Wash the peppers, remove the stalk, remove the seeds and cut into thin strips. Peel and chop the shallots and garlic. Carefully peel the ginger and chop very finely. Roast the coconut chips in a pan until light brown. Do this without fat. When they are light brown, remove them from the pan and set aside. Now add the noodles, peppers, shallots, garlic, ginger and frozen peas to the pan. Add the coconut milk, tomatoes, 300 ml water and 1 tsp salt. Bring to the boil with the lid on. Then simmer for about 12 minutes. Do not forget to stir until the noodles are al dente. Meanwhile, wash and drain the spinach and fold it into the finished pasta. Finally, season to taste with lime juice and sprinkle with coconut chips.

NOTES

Recipe 80: One-Pot Noodles Pak-Choi and Shiitake

Ingredients

- 4 - 6 mini pak choi (approx. 300 g)
- 120 g shiitake mushrooms
- 4 spring onions
- 1 clove of garlic
- 20 g ginger
- 200 g linguine (cooking time 7 - 9 min.)
- 4 - 5 tbsp. soy sauce
- 3 tbsp rice wine
- 1 tbsp rice vinegar
- 1 tsp dark sesame oil
- Salt
- Pepper
- 20 g cashew nuts (roasted and salted)

1. Wash and quarter the pak choi. Clean the mushrooms, preferably with kitchen paper, and cut into pieces as desired. Wash the spring onions, cut into rings and wash again. Peel and finely dice the ginger and garlic. Put the noodles and the prepared ingredients in a pan. Add 4 tbsp soy sauce with the rice wine and rice vinegar and 550 ml cold water. Add the sesame oil and stir. Add 0.5 tsp salt to this mixture. Cover the lid and bring to the boil. Simmer for approx. 10 - 12 minutes. Do not forget to stir. Add more liquid if necessary. When the noodles are al dente, season with soy sauce and pepper. Then roughly crush the cashew nuts and sprinkle over the top.

Recipe 81: One-Pot Pasta with Peppers, Vegan Feta and Walnuts

Ingredients

- 1 pepper, red
- 50 g dried tomatoes, in oil
- 200 g cherry tomatoes
- 1 red onion
- 1 clove of garlic
- 2 stalks basil
- 2 tbsp olive oil
- 200 g maccheroncini
- Salt
- 2 tbsp. Ajvar (paprika paste; from a jar)
- 30 g walnut kernels
- 100 g vegan feta
- Pepper

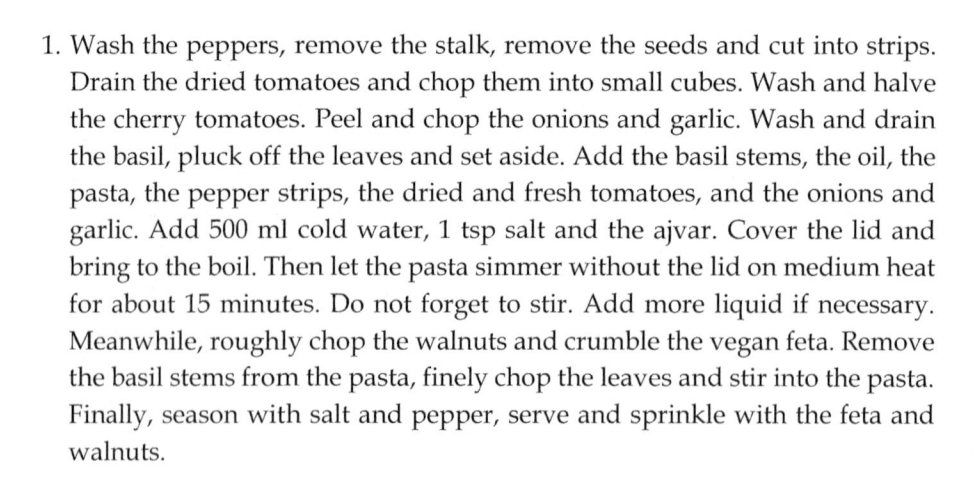

1. Wash the peppers, remove the stalk, remove the seeds and cut into strips. Drain the dried tomatoes and chop them into small cubes. Wash and halve the cherry tomatoes. Peel and chop the onions and garlic. Wash and drain the basil, pluck off the leaves and set aside. Add the basil stems, the oil, the pasta, the pepper strips, the dried and fresh tomatoes, and the onions and garlic. Add 500 ml cold water, 1 tsp salt and the ajvar. Cover the lid and bring to the boil. Then let the pasta simmer without the lid on medium heat for about 15 minutes. Do not forget to stir. Add more liquid if necessary. Meanwhile, roughly chop the walnuts and crumble the vegan feta. Remove the basil stems from the pasta, finely chop the leaves and stir into the pasta. Finally, season with salt and pepper, serve and sprinkle with the feta and walnuts.

Recipe 82: One-Pot Pasta with Fennel and Saffron

Saffron can work wonders: just a hint of the exquisite spice turns this pasta dish into a real golden delicacy!

Ingredients

- 1 pinch saffron threads
- 1 fennel bulb
- 1 onion
- 1 clove of garlic
- 1 red chilli pepper
- 2 - 3 stalks parsley
- 2 tbsp olive oil
- 200 g noodles.
- 1 tsp fennel seeds (coarsely crushed)
- 125 ml white wine
- Salt
- Pepper

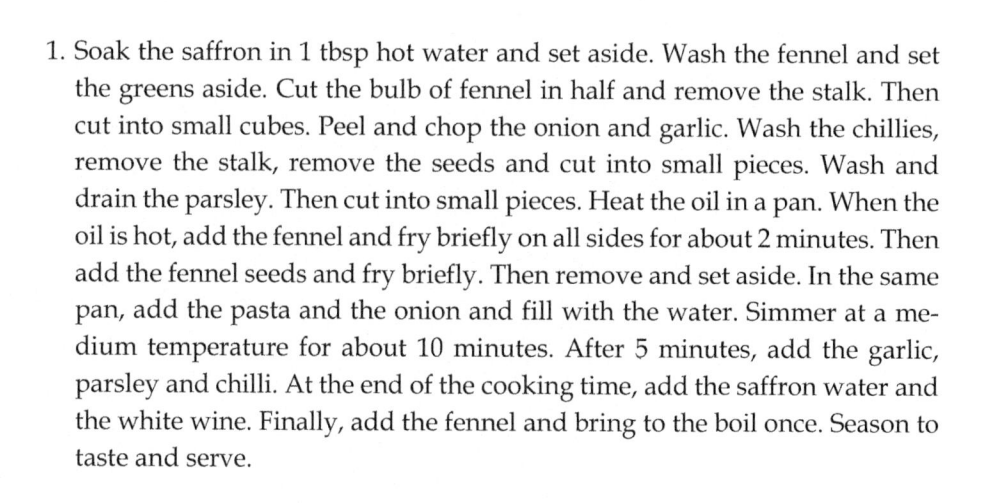

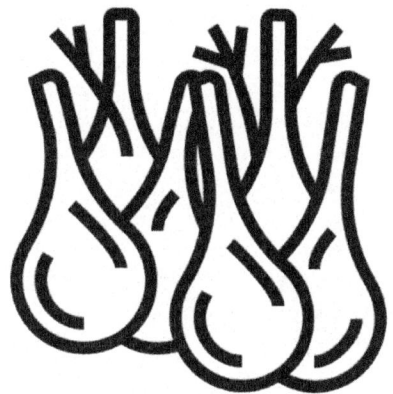

1. Soak the saffron in 1 tbsp hot water and set aside. Wash the fennel and set the greens aside. Cut the bulb of fennel in half and remove the stalk. Then cut into small cubes. Peel and chop the onion and garlic. Wash the chillies, remove the stalk, remove the seeds and cut into small pieces. Wash and drain the parsley. Then cut into small pieces. Heat the oil in a pan. When the oil is hot, add the fennel and fry briefly on all sides for about 2 minutes. Then add the fennel seeds and fry briefly. Then remove and set aside. In the same pan, add the pasta and the onion and fill with the water. Simmer at a medium temperature for about 10 minutes. After 5 minutes, add the garlic, parsley and chilli. At the end of the cooking time, add the saffron water and the white wine. Finally, add the fennel and bring to the boil once. Season to taste and serve.

Recipe 83: One-Pot Vegetable Pasta Green with Lemon Sauce

Ingredients

- 80 g sugar snaps
- 150 g green asparagus
- 1 bunch spring onions
- 2 stalks parsley
- 200 g green tagliatelle (cooking time 6 min.)
- 100 ml vegetable cream
- Salt
- grated zest of 1 organic lemon
- Pepper
- some lemon juice
- 1 handful chervil (alternatively parsley)

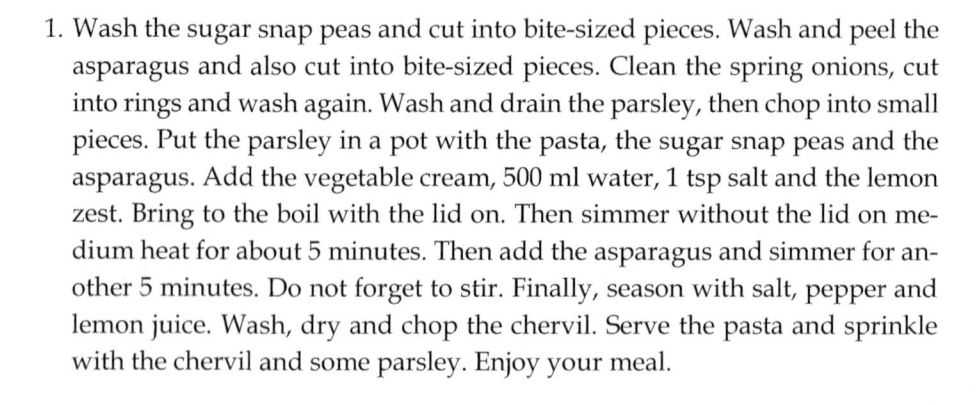

1. Wash the sugar snap peas and cut into bite-sized pieces. Wash and peel the asparagus and also cut into bite-sized pieces. Clean the spring onions, cut into rings and wash again. Wash and drain the parsley, then chop into small pieces. Put the parsley in a pot with the pasta, the sugar snap peas and the asparagus. Add the vegetable cream, 500 ml water, 1 tsp salt and the lemon zest. Bring to the boil with the lid on. Then simmer without the lid on medium heat for about 5 minutes. Then add the asparagus and simmer for another 5 minutes. Do not forget to stir. Finally, season with salt, pepper and lemon juice. Wash, dry and chop the chervil. Serve the pasta and sprinkle with the chervil and some parsley. Enjoy your meal.

Recipe 84: One-Pot Pasta with Artichokes

Ingredients

- 200 g cherry tomatoes
- 1 onion
- 1 clove of garlic
- 3 stalks parsley
- 1 tsp olive oil
- 200 g linguine (cooking time 7 - 9 min.)
- 100 ml white wine
- Salt
- 1 tsp dried oregano
- 120 g quartered artichoke hearts (from the jar)

For the pesto rosso:
- 30 g dried tomatoes (in oil)
- 1 ½ tbsp olive oil
- 15 g green olives, pitted
- 10 g pine nuts
- ¼ tsp chilli flakes
- 1 tbsp grated vegan hard cheese
- Salt
- Pepper

1. Wash the cherry tomatoes, remove the stalk and halve them. Peel and chop the onions and garlic. Wash and dry the parsley, pluck the leaves and chop them. Now heat some oil in a pan. When the oil is hot, add the pasta, onions, garlic, parsley stems and cherry tomatoes. Add the wine, 450 ml cold water, 1 tsp salt and the oregano. Bring everything to the boil with the lid on. Then simmer without the lid for about 12 minutes. Do not forget to stir. For the pesto rosso, drain the dried tomatoes. Cut them into small pieces. Blend with the oil, olives, 1 tbsp water, pine nuts and chilli flakes. Stir in the hard cheese. Finally, season with salt and pepper. Then drain the artichokes and cut them into smaller pieces if necessary. When the pasta is al dente, mix in the pesto, artichokes and parsley and mix well, season again. Then serve and garnish with the hard cheese and parsley. Enjoy it.

Recipe 85: One-Pot Plum Pasta, Sweet with Poppy Seeds

Ingredients

- 200 g mini croissant noodles (cooking time 6 min.)
- 400 ml vegetable milk
- Salt
- 1 strip of organic lemon zest (approx. 8 cm)
- 1 pkg. vanilla sugar
- 2 tablespoons sugar
- 40 g marzipan paste
- 120 g dried plums, pitted
- 2 tbsp ground poppy seeds

1. Put the pasta in a pan and heat it up. Add the milk, 300 ml cold water, a pinch of salt, the lemon zest, the vanilla sugar and 1 tbsp sugar. Wash, halve and stone the plums. Pluck the marzipan paste into approx. 1 cm pieces and add to the pan. Bring to the boil with the lid on. Then simmer without the lid for approx. 10 - 12 minutes. Do not forget to stir. When the pasta is al dente, remove the lemon peel and serve on deep plates. Then mix the poppy seeds and the remaining sugar and sprinkle over the top. Enjoy it.

NOTES

_____

_____

_____

Recipe 86: One-Pot Apple-Nut Penne with Raisins

Ingredients

- 2 tbsp planed hazelnuts
- 200 g penne (cooking time 5 min.)
- 40 g sultanas
- 400 ml vegetable milk
- Salt
- 2 - 3 pinches cinnamon powder
- 1 pkg. vanilla sugar
- 2 tablespoons sugar
- 2 red-skinned firm fleshed apples (180 g each; e.g. Jonagored)
- 2 tbsp vegetable cream

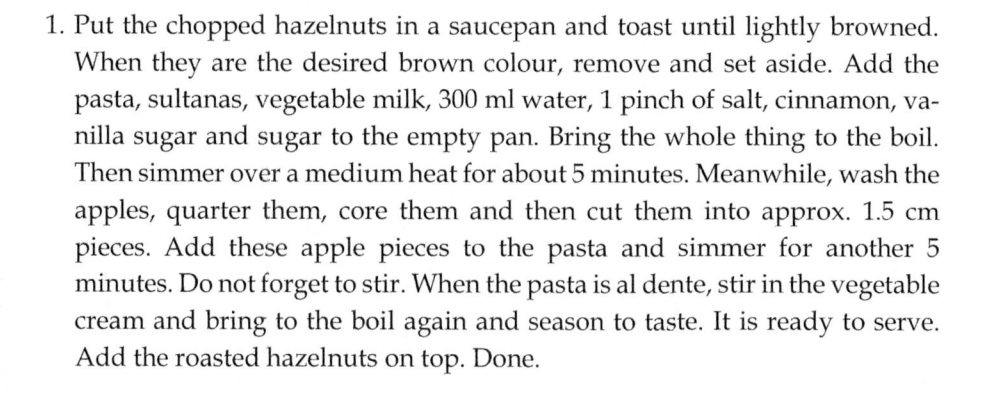

1. Put the chopped hazelnuts in a saucepan and toast until lightly browned. When they are the desired brown colour, remove and set aside. Add the pasta, sultanas, vegetable milk, 300 ml water, 1 pinch of salt, cinnamon, vanilla sugar and sugar to the empty pan. Bring the whole thing to the boil. Then simmer over a medium heat for about 5 minutes. Meanwhile, wash the apples, quarter them, core them and then cut them into approx. 1.5 cm pieces. Add these apple pieces to the pasta and simmer for another 5 minutes. Do not forget to stir. When the pasta is al dente, stir in the vegetable cream and bring to the boil again and season to taste. It is ready to serve. Add the roasted hazelnuts on top. Done.

Recipe 87: One-Pot Pasta TexMex with Avocado Salsa

Maize is an essential ingredient in Mexican cuisine. Here it is in the noodles. And its favourite partners such as minced meat, beans and oregano are sauce ingredients.

Ingredients

- 1 pepper, yellow
- 4 spring onions
- 1 clove of garlic
- 1 tablespoon olive oil
- 1 tsp dried oregano
- 200g vegan minced meat
- ½ tsp ground cumin
- 1 teaspoon sweet paprika powder
- approx. ½ tsp chilli flakes
- Salt
- 200 g gluten-free rigatoni (made from corn flour; cooking time 8 - 10 min.)
- 200 ml tomatoes (tin), chunky
- 1 small tin of kidney beans (140 g drained weight)

For the avocado salsa:
- 1 ripe avocado
- 2 - 3 tbsp lime juice
- 1 tomato (approx. 100 g)
- 1 handful coriander greens
- Salt
- approx. ¼ tsp chilli flakes

1. Wash the peppers, remove the stalk, remove the seeds and cut into small pieces. Clean the spring onion, cut into rings and wash again and drain. Peel and chop the garlic. Now put some oil in a pan and heat it. When the oil is hot, add the vegan mince and fry for about 3 minutes until crumbly. Add the oregano, cumin, paprika powder, chilli flakes and 1 tsp salt and fry briefly. Then remove the pan from the cooker. Add the noodles, peppers, spring onions and garlic. Add the tomatoes and 550 ml water. Put the pan back on the cooker and bring to the boil with the lid on. Then simmer without the lid for about 10-12 minutes. Do not forget to stir. Meanwhile, halve the avocado, remove the pit and peel the halves. Cut the flesh into small cubes and sprinkle with the lime juice. Wash the tomatoes, remove the stalk, cut them into quarters and remove the seeds. Now cut into small pieces and fold into the avocado. Wash, dry and roughly chop the coriander and mix into the avocado. Season with salt and chilli flakes. When the noodles are al dente, drain the kidney beans and mix them into the noodles just before the end of the cooking time. Serve with the salsa and enjoy.

Recipe 88: One-Pot Pasta Carrot Sage

Ingredients

- 300 g carrots
- 1 bunch spring onions
- 150 g cherry tomatoes
- 1 sprig rosemary
- approx. 12 sage leaves
- Olive oil
- 200 g buckwheat fusilli (cooking time 6 - 8 min.)
- Salt
- Pepper
- 80 g vegan feta

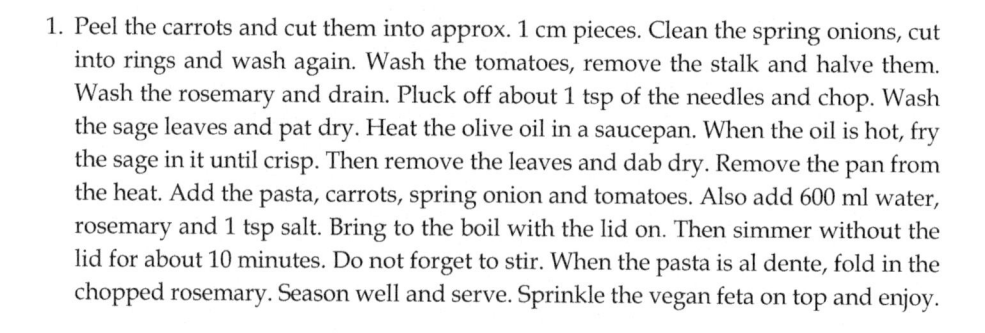

1. Peel the carrots and cut them into approx. 1 cm pieces. Clean the spring onions, cut into rings and wash again. Wash the tomatoes, remove the stalk and halve them. Wash the rosemary and drain. Pluck off about 1 tsp of the needles and chop. Wash the sage leaves and pat dry. Heat the olive oil in a saucepan. When the oil is hot, fry the sage in it until crisp. Then remove the leaves and dab dry. Remove the pan from the heat. Add the pasta, carrots, spring onion and tomatoes. Also add 600 ml water, rosemary and 1 tsp salt. Bring to the boil with the lid on. Then simmer without the lid for about 10 minutes. Do not forget to stir. When the pasta is al dente, fold in the chopped rosemary. Season well and serve. Sprinkle the vegan feta on top and enjoy.

Recipe 89: One-Pot Pasta with Peas and Mint

Ingredients

- 25 g pine nuts
- 1 handful parsley
- 2 stalks mint
- 1 organic lemon
- 200 g gluten-free spaghetti (e.g. made from corn and rice flour; cooking time 10 min.)
- 100 g frozen princess beans
- 150 g frozen peas
- 2 onions
- 650 ml vegetable stock
- Salt
- 1 tablespoon olive oil
- 1 clove of garlic
- Pepper

1. Peel and chop the onions and garlic. Wash and dry the parsley and mint. Pluck off the leaves and set aside. Wash the lemon hot, dry it and finely grate the peel. Set this aside too. Cut 2 slices from the lemon itself. Roast the pine nuts in a pan. When the desired brownness is reached, remove them. Now put the lemon slices in the pan, add the pasta, beans, peas and onions, as well as the stock, 0.5 tsp salt and the oil. Bring everything to the boil with the lid closed. Then let it simmer for about 10 - 12 minutes with the lid open. Do not forget to stir. Meanwhile, finely chop the garlic with the parsley leaves and the mint. Mix in the lemon zest. Remove the lemon slices from the pan, fold the parsley-mint-garlic mix into the pasta and season everything together again with salt, pepper and lemon juice. Serve on a plate and sprinkle with the pine nuts. Enjoy your meal.

Recipe 90: One-Pot Penne with Rutabaga and Peas

Ingredients

- 2 sprigs rosemary
- 150 g vegan hard cheese
- 250 ml vegetable stock
- 600 ml vegetable milk
- 200 g penne
- 200 g peas (frozen)
- ½ tsp salt
- 1 pinch of pepper

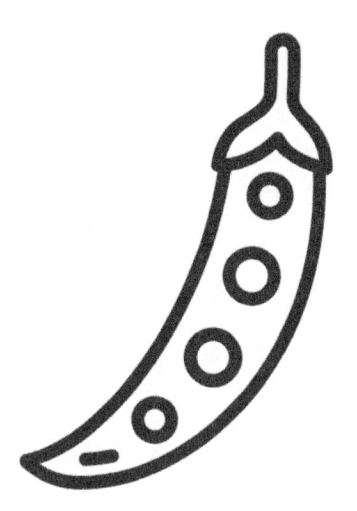

1. Peel the onions and cut them into small pieces. Peel the rutabaga and cut into 0.5 cm cubes. Wash and dry the rosemary and pluck off the needles. Then chop them into small pieces. Grate the vegan hard cheese. Put the rutabaga in a pot with the onions, rosemary and vegetable stock and simmer for about 15 - 20 minutes. When the vegetables are soft, mash everything with a potato masher. Then add the vegetable milk, vegan hard cheese, pasta, peas, salt and pepper. Simmer for about 10 minutes with the lid closed. Stir everything well. Finally, season again with salt and pepper and the dish is ready. Enjoy.

NOTES

Recipe 91: One-Pot Pasta with Vegan Feta, Pear and Chard

Ingredients

- 2 garlic cloves
- 2 pears
- 300 g chard
- 300 g vegan feta
- 4 tbsp walnuts
- 300 ml red wine
- 400 g farfalle

1. Peel and chop the garlic. Wash, peel and core the pears and cut into small cubes. Wash and dry the chard in the same way. Then cut into small pieces. Roughly dice the vegan feta and finely chop the walnuts. Put the garlic, pears, chard, feta and pasta in a pot and fill with red wine and 600 ml water. Bring to the boil with the lid on. Then simmer over medium heat for about 7 - 10 minutes. Stir well once more and serve. Finally, sprinkle with walnuts. Enjoy your meal.

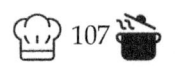

NOTES

Recipe 92: One-Pot Wholemeal Noodles with Pumpkin Curry Sauce

Ingredients

- 500 g Hokkaido pumpkin
- 1 onion
- 1 untreated lime
- Olive oil
- 2 tablespoons honey
- 1 tbsp curry powder
- ½ tsp chilli flakes
- 2 tbsp sultanas
- 450 ml vegetable cream
- 400 g wholemeal pasta
- Salt

1. Wash the pumpkin, remove the seeds and cut into small pieces. Peel and chop the onions. Wash the lime in hot water, dry it, grate the zest and squeeze out the juice. Heat the olive oil in a pot. When the oil is hot, sauté the onions for about 1 - 2 minutes. Then add the pumpkin pieces and sauté for another 5 minutes. Add the lime juice and zest, honey, curry powder, chilli flakes, sultanas, vegetable cream, noodles, a good pinch of salt and 800 ml water to the pot. Let the whole thing simmer over medium heat for about 10 - 15 minutes. Do not forget to stir. When the dish has the desired consistency, serve. Enjoy it.

NOTES

Recipe 93: One-Pot Red Cabbage Pasta

Ingredients

- 2 tbsp ketchup
- 7 tbsp olive oil
- 2 tablespoons honey
- 2 teaspoons sweet paprika powder
- Pepper
- 1 tablespoon mustard
- 2 tbsp. soy sauce
- 2 tablespoons Worcester sauce
- 350 g red cabbage
- 1 onion
- 1 clove of garlic
- 200 g short noodles

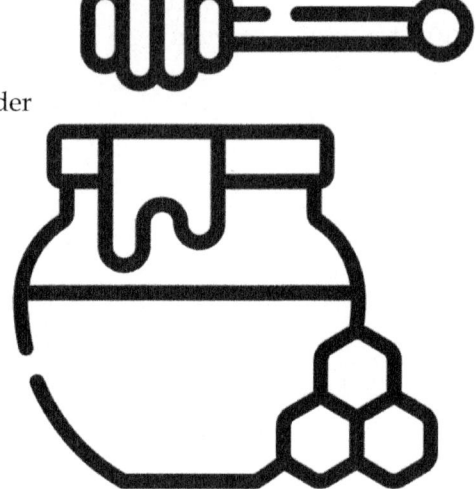

1. Peel and chop the onions and garlic. Mix the ketchup, 6 tbsp olive oil, honey, paprika powder, a pinch of pepper, mustard, soy sauce and Worcester sauce to make a marinade. Wash the red cabbage and cut into fine strips. Put the olive oil in a pot and heat it. When the oil is hot, sauté the garlic and onions in it. Then add the red cabbage and sauté briefly. Then stir in the marinade. Then add the pasta and 450 ml water. Bring everything to the boil once and then simmer without a lid over a medium heat for about 10 minutes. When the pasta is al dente, it is ready to serve. Enjoy it.

NOTES

_____

_____

Recipe 94: One-Pot Vegan Feta with Eggplant and Mint

Ingredients

- 600 g aubergine
- 2 onions
- 2 garlic cloves
- 200 g vegan feta
- 50 g walnuts
- 1 untreated lime
- 2-3 sprigs mint
- 2 tbsp olive oil
- 200 g peas (frozen)
- 400 g short noodles
- 800 ml vegetable stock
- ¼ tsp cayenne pepper
- 1 tsp curry powder
- Salt
- Pepper

1. Wash and chop the aubergines. Peel and chop the onions and garlic. Crumble the vegan feta cheese. Coarsely chop the walnuts. Rinse the lime in hot water, dry it, grate the zest and squeeze out the juice. Wash the mint, pluck off the leaves and chop finely. Heat the oil in a saucepan. When the oil is hot, sauté the onions and garlic. Then sauté the aubergines for about 3 minutes. Add the peas, noodles, lime juice and zest, half the feta, the stock and spices. Season with salt and pepper and simmer over medium heat with the lid on for about 10 minutes. When the pasta is al dente, it is ready to serve.

Recipe 95: One-Pot Pasta with Tomatoes, Olives and Artichokes

Ingredients

- 4 tbsp olives, green
- 200 g artichoke hearts from the jar
- 600 g tomatoes
- 1 onion
- 2 garlic cloves
- 2 tbsp olive oil
- 400 g short noodles
- 1 tsp salt
- 1 pinch of pepper
- 4 tbsp pine nuts

1. Drain and pit the olives and cut them into fine rings. Cut the artichoke hearts into fine strips. Wash the tomatoes, remove the stalk and finely dice. Peel and chop the onions and garlic. Put the oil in a pot and heat it. When the oil is hot, sauté the onions and garlic briefly. Then add the tomatoes, olives, artichoke hearts, pasta, salt and pepper to the pot. Pour in 600 ml of water and let everything simmer for about 8 - 10 minutes with the lid closed and over medium heat. Do not forget to stir. Meanwhile, roast the pine nuts in a small pan. Stir the pasta again, season to taste and serve. Sprinkle the pine nuts on top and enjoy.

NOTES

Recipe 96: One-Pot Rice Curry with Vegetables, Pineapple and Peanuts

Ingredients

- ½ pineapple
- 2 carrots
- 1 onion
- 100 g salted, roasted peanuts
- 200 g rice
- 200 g peas (frozen)
- 4 tsp sultanas
- 2-3 tbsp curry powder
- 1 tsp turmeric
- 1 tsp ground cumin
- 1 tsp. cinnamon powder
- ¼ tsp chilli powder
- 1 tsp salt
- 2 tbsp rapeseed oil

1. Peel the carrots and cut into cubes. Remove the skin from the pineapple and also cut into bite-sized cubes. Keep the juice. Peel and chop the onions. Chop the peanuts. Layer the rice, carrots, onion, pineapple, peas, sultanas, spices and salt in a pot. Pour the oil and pineapple juice over it and carefully add 300 ml water. Cover with a lid and let the curry simmer over medium heat for about 20-30 minutes. Then season again with salt and pepper and serve. Sprinkle the peanuts on the plate and enjoy.

NOTES

Recipe 97: One-Pot Kale - Rice - Pot

Ingredients

- 1 onion
- 800 g kale
- 4 dried tomatoes
- 150 g vegan hard cheese
- 2 tbsp olive oil
- 200 g rice
- 100 ml white wine
- 300 ml hot vegetable stock
- 1 tsp salt
- 1 pinch of pepper
- 2 tbsp pine nuts

1. Peel and chop the onion. Wash the kale. The hard ribs are not necessarily nice to eat and can be removed. Finely chop the leaves of the kale. Cut the dried tomatoes into fine strips. Grate the vegan hard cheese. Heat the oil in a saucepan. When the oil is hot, fry the onions, then add the rice and fry briefly. Then deglaze with the white wine and let it simmer briefly. Then add the kale, tomatoes, stock, hard cheese, salt and pepper and simmer over a medium heat with the lid on for about 20-30 minutes. Meanwhile, toast the pine nuts in a separate pan. When they are golden brown, the rice can be served and sprinkled with the pine nuts. Enjoy your meal.

NOTES

_____

_____

Recipe 98: One-Pot Curry Rice, Spicy with Beans

Ingredients

- 1 onion
- 3 garlic cloves
- 1 piece of ginger (approx. 1 cm)
- 1 chilli pepper
- 1 small bunch coriander
- 480 g canned kidney beans
- 1-2 tsp coriander seeds
- 1-2 tsp cumin seeds
- 1 tsp black sesame seeds
- Olive oil
- 200 g rice
- 250 g canned tomato pieces
- 1 tsp salt
- 1 tbsp agave syrup

1. Peel and chop the onion and garlic. Peel the ginger and chop finely. Wash the chilli pepper, remove the stalk, remove the seeds and chop finely. Wash, dry and finely chop the coriander. Wash the kidney beans and drain in a sieve. Crush the coriander, cumin and sesame seeds in a mortar. Heat the olive oil in a pot. When the oil is hot, toss the spices in it. Then add the onion and garlic and fry for about 1 minute. Then add the rice and mix it in. Then add the tomatoes, ginger, chilli, salt, honey and 300 ml water. Cover with a lid and simmer over medium heat for approx. 20 - 30 minutes. Stir occasionally. Before serving, add the chopped coriander and stir again thoroughly. Enjoy it.

Recipe 99: One-Pot Millet with Herbs and Green Asparagus

Ingredients

- 1 kg asparagus, green
- 3 spring onions
- 1 bunch of mixed herbs (e.g. wild garlic, chervil, parsley, chives, sorrel)
- 250 g millet
- 700 ml hot vegetable stock
- 100 ml vegetable cream
- Salt
- Pepper

1. Wash and peel the asparagus. Check for woody parts and remove them. Then cut into bite-sized pieces. Clean the spring onions, cut into rings and then wash again. Wash and dry the herbs, then chop finely. Put the millet in a sieve and rinse hot. Then put it in a pot with the asparagus, spring onions, stock and vegetable cream and simmer for about 20 minutes with the lid closed on medium heat. Do not forget to stir. At the end of the cooking time, mix in the herbs and season again with salt and pepper. It is ready to be served.

NOTES

_____

_____

Recipe 100: One-Pot Chard Bulgur Eggplant & Pomegranate

Finally, a One-Pot, which is a little unusual.

Ingredients

- 1 aubergine
- 500 g chard
- 3 garlic cloves
- 3 spring onions
- 1 pomegranate
- 600 ml hot vegetable stock
- 300 g bulgur
- Salt
- Pepper
- 2 tbsp roasted sesame oil

1. Wash the aubergine and cut into approx. 1 cm cubes. Wash and clean the chard. Finely dice the stems and cut the leaves into fine strips. Peel and chop the garlic. Clean the spring onions, cut into rings and wash again. Remove the seeds from the pomegranate, reserving the juice. Put the bulgur, aubergine, chard, garlic, half the spring onions, pomegranate juice and vegetable stock in a pot and bring to the boil. Cover with a lid and leave to soak over a medium heat for about 20 minutes. Season with salt and pepper and stir well. Serve and garnish with the rest of the spring onions and the pomegranate seeds and sesame oil. Enjoy it.

NOTES

_____

_____

ONE POT
VEGAN EASY & TASTY

Spread

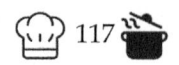

Recipe 101: Almond Puree

Ingredients:

- 500 gram unpeeled almonds
- a pinch of cinnamon

Preparation:

1. First, preheat the oven to 150 degrees and then roast the almonds on a baking tray for about 5 minutes - then the almonds should cool down a bit.
2. Take a blender and puree the almonds on the lowest setting. Then add the cinnamon. Pause for a moment and blend again for about 1 ½ minutes, but now on a higher setting. Repeat the process until you have a creamy almond paste.

Recipe 102: Nut spread

Ingredients:

- 200 gram cashew nuts
- 1 tbsp. oil
- 1 tsp lemon juice
- 100 gram apple syrup

Preparation:

1. Puree all the ingredients in a food processor or with a hand blender to a homogeneous mixture.
2. Fill the finished nut spread into preserving jars and the delicious spread is ready!

Recipe 103: Jam Without Sugar

Ingredients:

- 300 grams of any fruit
- a sachet of agar- agar
- 150 ml apple juice

Preparation:

1. Puree the peeled and seeded fruit of your choice and then gradually add the apple juice and agar-agar - then mix everything together well.
2. Now put everything together in a pot and boil it down to a thick mixture.
3. Then fill the finished jam into jars. Turn the jars upside down for about 3 minutes, then turn them over and let them cool. Closed, the jam will keep for up to four weeks - opened, however, it will only keep for seven days in the fridge.

Recipe 104: Apricot Jam

Ingredients:

- 250 grams soft apricots
- 70 ml orange juice without added sugar
- 30 ml water

Preparation:

1. Puree all ingredients finely with a blender or hand blender.
2. Now fill the mixture into a preserving jar and store it in the refrigerator. It is best to use the jam within a week.

Recipe 105: Date Cream

Ingredients:

- 100 grams ground hazelnuts
- 80 ml water
- 75 grams unsulphured dates
- 1- 2 tbsp. carob
- Vanilla to taste
- 2 tablespoons coconut oil

Preparation:

1. Soak the dates overnight.
2. Put all the ingredients in a tall container and mix everything well with a hand blender. Mix until you get a creamy mixture. If the cream is too dry, you can also add a little water.
3. The spread will keep refrigerated for up to two weeks.

Recipe 106: Peanut Puree

Ingredients:

- 1 tbsp agave syrup
- 2 tablespoons peanut oil
- 220 grams peanuts

Preparation:

1. Roast the peanuts in a pan without oil. Then let them cool down a little.
2. Chop the nuts, oil and agave syrup in a food processor or with a hand blender. Then fill the finished puree into a jar and leave the mixture to set in the fridge.

Recipe 107: Hummus with Avocado

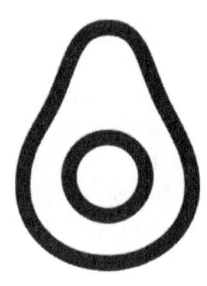

Ingredients:
(for approx. 150 grams of hummus)

- 300 grams cooked chickpeas incl. broth
- 2 tbsp. lemon juice
- 3 tbsp olive oil
- One very ripe avocado
- ½ tsp ground coriander

Preparation:

1. First cook the chickpeas, pass them through a sieve and catch the broth - keep it.
2. Then puree the chickpeas with the lemon juice, olive oil, ground coriander and 3 tablespoons of stock.
3. Then add the avocado flesh and puree it as well. Then add the chickpea broth until the perfect hummus consistency is achieved.

Recipe 108: Coconut-Banana Spread

Ingredients:
(for six servings)

- 150 grams grated coconut
- 40 grams coconut oil
- Three ripe bananas
- 1 tablespoon lemon juice
- A pinch of ground cinnamon

Preparation:

1. Peel the bananas and roughly chop them. Then mash the bananas to a pulp with a fork.
2. Heat the coconut oil over medium heat and stir it into the banana mash.
3. Now add the rest of the ingredients to the mashed bananas - you should stir until you get a creamy mixture.

Recipe 109: Jerusalem Artichoke Tuber Spread

Ingredients:
(for two servings)

- 4 tbsp. sunflower oil
- 5 tbsp (homemade) almond paste
- 1 ½ tbsp Jerusalem artichoke powder
- Vanilla powder to taste
- 1 ½ tbsp. carob powder

Preparation:

1. Stir the almond paste and oil in a bowl until smooth. Then add the Jerusalem artichoke and carob and mix everything together.
2. If you like, you can add some vanilla powder and season the spread accordingly.

ONE POT

VEGAN EASY & TASTY

Bread

Recipe 110: Chia Spelt Bread

Ingredients for 1 loaf:
- 500 g wholemeal spelt flour
- 130 g sunflower seeds
- 20 g chia seeds
- Salt
- 1 sachet dry yeast
- 2 tablespoons apple cider vinegar
- 500 ml water

Also: box baking tin (28 cm long) or similar

Preparation:
1. Mix all the dry ingredients together in a bowl.
2. Add the water and apple vinegar and mix with a hand mixer (dough hook) until a smooth dough form.
3. Line or grease a loaf tin with baking paper and sprinkle with flour. Spread the dough evenly in the tin. Place the loaf tin in a cold oven on the middle shelf. Now heat the oven to 200 degrees top and bottom heat and bake the bread for 1 hour. Then remove the bread from the oven. After cooling, turn the bread out of the loaf tin.

Recipe 111: Farmhouse bread

Ingredients for 1 loaf:
- 10 g organic fresh baker's yeast
- 300 g organic wholemeal wheat flour
- 150 g organic wheat flour
- 60 g organic spelt flour
- 50 g wholemeal rye sourdough, dry
- 10 g salt

Also:
Cast iron pot with lid

Preparation:
1. Dissolve the yeast in 400 ml lukewarm water. Knead the different types of flour, wholemeal rye sourdough powder and the water-yeast mixture with the dough hook of a hand mixer for 5 minutes. Let the dough rest for 20 minutes.
2. Add the salt and knead the dough for another 5 minutes until it comes away easily from the edge of the bowl. Leave to rise for 1 hour. Fold to the centre with a dough scraper every 15 minutes. This will trap extra air in the dough.
3. Line a large bowl with a towel and flour it really well. Turn the dough out onto a floured work surface. With slightly moistened hands, fold all four sides from the outside in. Place in the lined bowl with the resulting seal seam facing upwards and leave covered to rise for 30 minutes. Meanwhile, preheat the pan in the oven to the highest setting (250 degrees top/- and bottom heat).
4. Remove the pan from the oven. Turn the dough out of the bowl into the pot. Hold the cloth while doing this. Put the lid on and bake in the oven. The bread is ready when it sounds hollow when tapped.

ONE POT
VEGAN EASY & TASTY

Snacks

Recipe 112: Sheet Pan Kale Crisps

Ingredients for 4 servings:

Preparation time: approx. 50 minutes

- 250 grams kale
- 1 teaspoon chilli flakes, dried
- 2 teaspoons herb salt
- 40 ml olive oil

Preparation:

1. First preheat the oven to 130 degrees.
2. Wash the kale, dry it and remove the stalk. Cut the kale into bite-sized pieces (not too small, the kale shrinks in the oven).
3. Mix the oil with the salt and chilli flakes in a bowl and toss the kale pieces. The kale should be well covered with the oil.
4. Now spread the pieces on a baking tray covered with baking paper. Bake in the preheated oven for approx. 30 - 40 minutes. Open the oven door from time to time so that the steam can escape.
5. The chips are also delicious when served with a herb dip.

Recipe 113: Vanilla Cinnamon Almond Snack

Ingredients for 2 servings:

- 50 g almonds
- 1 tablespoon coconut oil
- 1 tsp ground vanilla
- 1 pinch cinnamon

Preparation:

1. Heat 1 tsp coconut oil in a pan.
2. Toast the almonds for 3 minutes over medium heat. Add the cinnamon and ground vanilla, mix together and roast for about 1 minute.
3. Leave the roasted almonds to cool on a baking tray lined with baking paper.
4. Enjoy as a delicious snack.

Recipe 114: Hummus with Vegetable Sticks

Ingredients for 2 servings:
- 300 g canned chickpeas
- 1 garlic clove
- Juice of 1/2 lemon
- 2 tbsp olive oil
- 2 tbsp tahini (sesame paste)
- Salt/ Pepper
- 1 tsp chilli powder
- 1 tsp paprika powder

Sticks:
- 1 carrot/ 1 cucumber
- 1 stalk of celery

Preparation:
1. Drain the chickpeas from the tin and add the lemon juice and garlic cloves and puree everything together.
2. Once everything is well pureed, add the sesame seeds. Season to taste with salt, pepper, paprika powder and chilli powder.
3. For dipping, wash and clean the vegetables and cut into strips.

Recipe 115: Sesame Sunflower Crackers

Ingredients for 20 crackers:

- 125 g sunflower seeds
- 70 g sesame seeds
- 1 clove of garlic
- 1 tbsp dried herbs (e.g. rosemary)
- 3-5 tbsp. water
- 1 tablespoon olive oil
- ¼ tsp salt

Preparation:
1. Preheat the oven to 180 degrees top and bottom heat.
2. Grind the sunflower seeds, salt and garlic in a blender or food processor on high speed for a few minutes until the whole thing looks slightly flour-like.
3. Add the sesame seeds, herbs and olive oil and mix on a low heat.
4. Add water by the spoonful until the mixture reaches a doughy consistency.
5. Roll out on a baking tray with baking paper. It is best to place another sheet of baking paper on top of the dough and then flatten with a rolling pin. Cut into pieces with a knife.
6. Bake for 10-15 minutes or until the crackers are lightly brown around the edges.
7. Allow to cool completely and then break apart.

Recipe 116: Cinnamon Crispy Flakes

Ingredients for 2 servings:
Preparation time: approx. 5 minutes

- 250 ml vegetable milk
- 1 tablespoon cinnamon, ground
- 2 tablespoons maple syrup
- 8 crispy breads e.g. Leicht & Cross or Filinchen

Preparation:
1. First, chop the crispbread into coarse pieces.
2. Mix the maple syrup and cinnamon in a bowl and fold in the crunchy bits.
3. Prepare two bowls of milk and divide the crispy flakes evenly.
4. Serve with fresh fruit if desired.

Recipe 117: Vegan Porridge with Vanilla

Ingredients for 4 servings:
Preparation time: approx. 15 minutes

- 200 g tender oat flakes
- 1 tablespoon bourbon vanilla, ground
- 1 pinch cinnamon, ground
- 2 tablespoons maple syrup
- 850 ml rice or oat milk
- Topping: e.g. strawberries, bananas, blueberries, apples, nuts, chia seeds

Preparation:
1. Put the oat flakes, cinnamon, vanilla and maple syrup in a pot with the milk. Bring to the boil and remove from the heat. Cover and leave to soak for about 10 minutes.
2. In the meantime, you can prepare the topping. Cut the fruit of your choice into bite-sized pieces.
3. Divide the finished porridge into four portions, garnish with the topping and serve immediately.

Recipe 118: Vegan Strawberry Banana Smoothie

Ingredients for 2 servings:
Preparation time: approx. 5 minutes
- 4 bananas
- 250 grams strawberries
- 1 pinch cinnamon, ground
- 1 tablespoon agave syrup
- 4 tablespoons linseed, coarsely ground
- 500 ml almond or rice milk

Preparation:
1. Put all the ingredients in a blender and blend until creamy. If the smoothie is too thick, just add some milk and blend briefly.

Recipe 119: Raspberry Smoothie

Ingredients for 2 servings:
Preparation time: approx. 5 minutes
- 200 g frozen raspberries
- 1 pinch cinnamon, ground
- 2 tablespoons agave syrup or honey
- 2 tablespoons tender oat flakes
- 400 ml vegetable milk

Preparation:
1. Put all the ingredients in a blender and blend until creamy. If the smoothie is too thick, add a little more milk.

Recipe 120: Breakfast Smoothie

Ingredients for 1 serving:
Preparation time: approx. 5 minutes

- 1 ripe banana
- 1 tablespoon tender oat flakes
- 1 tablespoon wheat germ
- 250 ml plant milk

Preparation:

1. Put all the ingredients in a blender and blend until creamy. This smoothie is perfect if your child doesn't want to eat breakfast in the morning. You can add variety by varying the fruit. Use raspberries, strawberries, blueberries etc.

Recipe 121: Vegan Pick-Me-Up Smoothie

Ingredients for 3 servings:
Preparation time: approx. 30 minutes

- 1 ripe papaya
- 2 tablespoons chia seeds
- 1 pinch cinnamon, ground
- 1 tablespoon coconut blossom sugar
- 800 ml coconut rice drink
- 400 ml hazelnut drink

Preparation:

1. First, mix the hazelnut milk and the coconut rice milk with the quinoa. Add the cinnamon and coconut blossom sugar and stir well. Let everything soak for about 20 minutes, stirring in between.
2. In the meantime, peel the papaya, remove the seeds and cut it into small pieces.
3. Finally, put the papaya and the milk-quinoa mixture into a blender and blend until creamy.

Recipe 122: Good Morning Soup

Ingredients for 1 serving:
Preparation time: approx. 15 minutes

- 50 grams tender oat flakes
- 1 pinch of salt
- 2 tablespoons honey or agave syrup
- 300 ml vegetable milk

Preparation:

1. First, bring the milk to the boil. Reduce the heat and stir in the oat flakes, salt and honey and simmer for about 10 minutes. Stir regularly.
2. The soup will be rather thick. If you want it to be more liquid, add a little milk.

Recipe 123: Quick Semolina Porridge

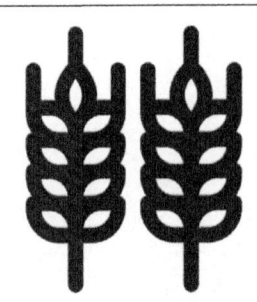

Ingredients for 2 servings:
Preparation time: approx. 10 minutes

- 90 grams semolina
- 1 pinch cinnamon, ground
- 3 tablespoons sugar, honey or agave syrup
- 500 ml plant milk
- Topping: cocoa powder, butter

Preparation:

1. First, put the milk, semolina, cinnamon and sugar in a saucepan and simmer over medium heat until the mixture thickens. Keep stirring so that the porridge doesn't burn.
2. If the porridge is too solid, simply add a little more milk. If it is too liquid, stir in a little semolina and let the porridge swell a little.
3. Now divide the porridge into two portions and refine it with cocoa powder and butter. Best enjoyed hot.

ONE POT
VEGAN EASY & TASTY

Dessert

Recipe 124: Coconut Semolina Porridge

Ingredients for 2 servings:
Preparation time: approx. 20 minutes
- 150 grams semolina
- 2 tablespoons honey or sugar
- 400 ml coconut milk
- 200 ml water
- For garnish: 2 tablespoons grated coconut

Preparation:

1. Bring the coconut milk and water to the boil in a saucepan and reduce the heat.
2. Stir in the honey and semolina and let everything simmer while stirring until the porridge becomes more solid.
3. Serve in two bowls and garnish with grated coconut.

Recipe 125: After-Eight Chocolate Cream

Ingredients for 4 servings:
Preparation time: approx. 10 minutes
- 4 ripe avocados
- 4 ripe bananas
- 3 sprigs mint
- 120 grams cocoa powder
- 2 tablespoons honey or agave syrup
- For garnish: 4 tablespoons nuts, chopped

Preparation:

1. First peel the avocados and bananas and puree them together with the mint leaves using a hand blender.
2. Stir in the cocoa powder and honey.
3. Leave to infuse in the fridge for at least one hour.
4. Garnish with chopped nuts before serving.

Recipe 126: Berry Semolina Porridge

Ingredients for 3 servings:
Preparation time: approx. 15 minutes

- 140 grams semolina
- 200 g frozen berry mix
- 2 ripe bananas
- 2 tablespoons honey or agave syrup
- 600 ml plant milk (e.g. almond milk)

Preparation:

1. First put the milk and honey in a saucepan, bring to the boil briefly and stir in the semolina. Simmer over reduced heat, stirring, for about 5 minutes.
2. Peel the banana and mash it with a fork. Then fold the banana into the semolina porridge.
3. Divide the semolina porridge into four portions. Garnish with berries before serving.

Recipe 127: Banana Chia Pudding

Ingredients for 2 servings:
Preparation time: approx. 3 hours with cooling time

- 90 grams chia seeds
- 2 ripe bananas
- 2 tablespoons honey or agave syrup
- 3 tablespoons cocoa powder
- 400 ml plant milk (e.g. rice-coconut drink)
- To garnish: 1 handful of berries

Preparation:

1. First mix the milk, cocoa and honey in a bowl and stir in the chia seeds.
2. Peel the banana and cut into thin slices. Fold into the mixture and leave to soak in the fridge for at least 3 hours.
3. Divide the pudding into two portions and garnish with the berries before serving.

Recipe 128: Express Dessert Chocolate Banana

Ingredients for 4 servings:
Preparation time: approx. 5 minutes

- 4 bananas
- 2 tablespoons baking cocoa
- 2 tablespoons honey or agave syrup
- 2 tablespoons water

Preparation:

1. First cut the bananas lengthwise and place the banana halves on a plate.
2. Now mix the baking cocoa with the water, slowly stirring in the water. Add the honey to this sauce. Pour the chocolate sauce over the banana halves and heat in the microwave for about 10 seconds. Your lightning dessert is ready.

Recipe 129: Vegan Raw Food Dessert

Ingredients for 4 servings:
Preparation time: approx. 15 minutes

- 4 apples
- 4 carrots
- Juice from 2 oranges
- 2 tablespoons agave syrup
- 1 tablespoon oil to taste
- 1 tablespoon fine oat flakes
- For garnish: 1 orange

Preparation:

1. First peel and finely grate the carrots, then finely grate the apples.
2. Mix the grated carrots and apples with the orange juice, oil, honey and oat flakes in a bowl.
3. Peel the orange and cut it into thin slices.
4. Garnish with the sliced orange before serving.

Recipe 130: Colourful Fruit Island

Ingredients for 4 servings:
Preparation time: approx. 10 minutes
- 8 blueberries
- 4 kiwis
- 2 bananas
- 2 oranges
- some lemon juice

Preparation:
1. First peel the kiwis, oranges and bananas. Cut the kiwis into slices and halve them, divide the oranges into wedges and halve the bananas lengthwise.
2. On a large plate, make the bottom of the island out of the orange wedges. The banana halves are the palm tree trunks, the kiwi slices are the palm tree leaves and the blueberries are the coconuts.
3. Finally, drizzle a little lemon juice over the banana halves to prevent them from turning brown.

Recipe 131: Vegan Chocolate Porridge

Ingredients for 2 servings:
- 90 grams tender oat flakes
- 300 ml hazelnut milk/almond milk
- 1 tbsp maple syrup
- A pinch of cinnamon
- 1 tbsp cocoa powder

Topping:
- One banana and 1 tbsp chopped nuts

Preparation:
1. Take a pot and mix the oat flakes, cocoa, cinnamon, maple syrup and milk together. Bring everything to the boil and then take the pot off the cooker to let the mixture swell for about 10 minutes, covered.
2. Now the finished porridge can be divided into two portions and put into bowls. Finally, add the sliced banana and the chopped nuts as a topping to the porridge. Enjoy it now!

Recipe 132: Waffles with Coconut

Ingredients:
(approx. 6 waffles)
- 65 grams soft, dried apricots
- 100 ml oat milk
- 180 gram spelt flour
- 1 tsp baking powder
- 200 g coconut milk
- 50 gram coconut oil

Preparation:
1. Put the apricots, coconut milk, coconut oil and oat milk in a pot and heat everything for about 6 minutes.
2. Puree everything with a hand blender or stand mixer.
3. Now add the coconut flakes, flour and baking powder to the pureed ingredients. Now pour the finished batter into a waffle iron.

Recipe 133: Fruit Bar

Ingredients:
- 75 ml pure fruit juice (apple, grape, orange, etc.)
- 100 g oat flakes/ almond flour/ cornflakes
- Optional: 40 grams nuts
- Baking wafers
- 250 g unsulphured dried fruit of your choice

Preparation:
1. Put all the above ingredients in a blender and puree everything to a fine paste.
2. Take two wafers for each fruit bar and spread one half with the fruit mixture. Then fold the other half on top.
3. Then place the finished fruit bars on a board and another board on top of the bars so that they stick together nicely without the wafers curling.

ONE POT
VEGAN EASY & TASTY

Ice

Recipe 134: Banana Ice Cream

Ingredients:

- one large and ripe banana
- three ice sticks

Preparation:

1. Cut the peeled banana into three pieces.
2. Now skewer the three pieces on the sticks and put the banana skewers in the freezer for about two hours. After that it can be enjoyed.

Recipe 135: Melon Ice Cream

Ingredients:

- a large watermelon
- Ice cream sticks

Preparation:

1. Cut the watermelon into thick slices.
2. Now cut the slices into eighths.
3. Now you can cut a slit in the shell with a knife where you can insert the chopstick.
4. Afterwards, all the finished watermelons can be placed in the freezer with the ice cream stick for at least 6 hours.

Recipe 136: Avocado Ice Cream

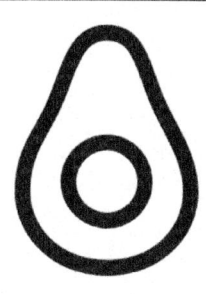

Ingredients:

- 400 ml coconut milk
- 1 ½ avocado
- Coconut flakes
- 4 tbsp agave syrup
- the juice of one lime

Preparation:

1. Beat the creamy coconut milk mixture with a hand mixer until creamy.
2. Now halve the avocados, remove the pit so that you can easily take out the flesh and put it in a bowl.
3. Gradually pour the lime juice over the avocados and mix together until creamy.
4. Now fold the avocado with the lime and the agave syrup or another sweetener of your choice into the whipped coconut milk.
5. Now put the finished ice cream mixture into a smaller bowl or baking dish and cover it with cling film. After about 5 hours in the freezer, the mixture should have turned into a delicious ice cream.

Recipe 137: Mango-Pineapple-Coconut Ice Cream

Ingredients:

- 150 ml coconut milk
- 1 tbsp maple syrup
- 80 grams mango
- 80 grams pineapple
- Half a banana
- A pinch of vanilla
- A dash of lemon juice

Preparation:

1. Puree the peeled and chopped mango, banana and pineapple with a blender or in a blender.
2. Add the creamy coconut milk, maple syrup, vanilla and dash of lemon juice to the pureed mixture and mix together.
3. Now the ice cream mixture can be filled into ice cream moulds and placed in the freezer for about three hours.

Recipe 138: Raspberry Banana Ice Cream

Ingredients:
(four servings)
- 300 g frozen raspberries
- Three bananas
- Half a litre of water

Preparation:

1. Cut the bananas into small pieces and mash them with the raspberries and the water, which you should add little by little so that the mixture does not become too liquid.
2. Now everything can be placed in the freezer for a few hours. Meanwhile, it is good to stir the mixture several times.

Recipe 139: Fruit Lollipops

Ingredients:
- Any fruit, e.g. kiwi, melon, mango
- short skewers/straws

Preparation:

1. Cut the fruit of your choice into 1 cm pieces.
2. Then skewer the cut fruit on a short skewer, which should not be pointed, or on a short straw.
3. The skewers can now already be enjoyed or you can put them in the freezer for a few more hours.

Recipe 140: Kiwi Popsicle

Ingredients:
(for 8 ice cream moulds)
- 7 Kiwis
- 1 lime

Popsicle moulds with handle

Preparation:

1. Clean & peel the kiwis. Cut one kiwi into very thin slices. Squeeze the lime well.
2. Puree the remaining kiwi with the lime juice.
3. Place the kiwi slices in ice-cream moulds. Pour the fruit puree into the moulds and place in the freezer for 40 minutes. Then place popsicle sticks in the centre of the ice cream. Leave the ice cream to freeze for at least 3 hours.

Recipe 141: Capri Ice Cream a la Casa

Ingredients:
(for 6 ice cream moulds)
- 600 ml orange juice
- 1/2 lime

Popsicle moulds with handle

Preparation:

1. Squeeze the lime well and mix with the orange juice.

Put everything into the ice-cream moulds and put them in the freezer over night.

Recipe 142: Berry Ice Cream

Ingredients:

- 250 grams frozen berries
- 300 grams yoghurt
- 1 tbsp maple syrup

Preparation:

1. Puree the berries after you have let them thaw a little.
2. Then add the yoghurt and maple syrup and mix everything together well.
3. Pour the mixture into a suitable bowl and place it in the freezer for at least three hours. Again, stir the ice cream several times.

NOTES

ONE POT
VEGAN EASY & TASTY

Drinks

Recipe 143: Herb-Ginger-Spice Tea

Ingredients for 4 glasses:

- 80 g ginger
- 1 bunch sage
- 2 sprigs rosemary
- 1 organic lemon
- 2 Star anise
- 1 cinnamon stick

Preparation:

1. Peel the ginger and cut into thin slices, wash the sage and rosemary thoroughly, wash the lemon with hot water, halve it and cut off three thin slices.
2. Put the ginger, herbs, star anise, cinnamon stick and lemon in a teapot. Fill with 1 litre of boiling hot water. Let everything steep for 6-8 minutes, then strain and sip. Can be enjoyed hot or cold.

Recipe 144: Infused Water

Ingredients for 8 glasses:

- 50 g ginger
- 200 g organic cucumber
- 1 organic orange
- 1 pomegranate
- 1 bunch mint
- 2 L mineral water

Preparation:

1. Wash the ingredients and peel if necessary. Slice the ginger, cucumber and 'orange. Remove the pomegranate seeds. Pluck the mint. Put everything in a carafe, fill with mineral water and chill for 2 hours.

Recipe 145: Pineapple-Lime Drink

Ingredients for 4 glasses:

- 500 g pineapple
- 1 Apple
- 2 organic limes
- 125 g organic raspberries, frozen
- 500 ml mineral water

Preparation:

1. Peel the pineapple, remove the stalk and cut into small pieces. Wash and quarter the apple. Then remove the core and cut the apple quarters into pieces.
2. Wash the limes under running hot water, finely puree the pineapple and apple cubes together with the water using a blender. Add the juice of one lime and fill into glasses together with some ice cubes.
3. Cut the second lime into thin slices and garnish the glasses with them. Lightly press on the frozen raspberries and place them on top.

Recipe 146: Lemon Ginger Lemonade

Ingredients for 4 glasses:

- 1 litre mineral water
- 3 tbsp ginger juice
- 2 lemons
- 15 ice cubes

Preparation:

1. Pour the mineral water into a large carafe and add the ginger juice.
2. Squeeze the lemons and stir in the juice.
3. Add ice cubes and enjoy.

Recipe 147: Peach Iced Tea

Ingredients for 4 glasses:

- 1 litre water
- 3 bags rooibos tea
- 4 peaches
- 15 ice cubes

Preparation:

1. Cut three of the four peaches into small pieces.
2. Pour boiling water into the tea bag and add the peach pieces. Let the tea steep according to the instructions.
3. Remove the tea bags after the specified time and leave the rest in the fridge with half the ice cubes for a good 1 hour.
4. Then remove the peach pieces again and fill up with the remaining ice cubes. Cut the last peach freshly into wedges and divide among the glasses.
5. If necessary, sweeten with peach juice and decorate with mint or lemon balm.

Recipe 148: Pomegranate Lemonade

Ingredients for 4 glasses:

- 1 pomegranate
- 1 lemon
- 1 litre
- 2 sprigs mint
- 8 ice cubes

Preparation:

1. Cut the pomegranate in half and juice each half with a lemon squeezer. Then squeeze the lemon.
2. In a jug, mix the pomegranate juice with the juice of the lemon. Also add a few pomegranate seeds.
3. Add a litre of mineral water and serve with 2 ice cubes per glass and a few mint leaves.

Recipe 149: Cucumber-Mint Lemonade

Ingredients for 4 glasses:

- 1 bunch mint
- 1 medium organic lemon
- 1/2 medium cucumber
- 1000 ml water
- 8 ice cubes

Preparation:

1. Wash the mint.
2. Wash the cucumber and lemon thoroughly and cut into slices.
3. Mix the cucumber and lemon slices with about 4 mint stalks and the water in a carafe. Leave to infuse.
4. Fill glasses each with 2 ice cubes and 1 stem of mint and top up with the cucumber lemonade, fish a few slices of cucumber from the carafe and add.

Recipe 150: Strawberry and Rosehip Iced Tea

Ingredients for 4 glasses:

- 1000 ml water
- 3 bags rose hip tea
- 1 medium lime(s)
- 100 g strawberry(s)
- 15 ice cubes

Preparation:

1. Boil the rosehip tea according to the instructions and then leave to cool.
2. Pour the tea into a jug with half the ice cubes and place in the fridge for a good 1 hour.
3. Squeeze the lime and add the juice.
4. Slice the strawberries and the other half of the lime and add to the tea with the remaining ice cubes.

Recipe 151: Orange-Lemon Iced Tea

Ingredients for 4 glasses:
- 1000 ml water
- 3 green tea bags
- 16 ice cubes
- 1 medium orange(s) (organic)
- 1 medium lemon(s) (organic)
- 1/2 medium lime(s)

Preparation:
1. Prepare the tea according to the instructions. Then remove the tea bags and allow the tea to cool.
2. Put the tea in a jug with half the ice cubes and chill in the fridge for about an hour.
3. In the meantime, cut the orange and lemon into thin slices. Squeeze the lime.
4. After the tea has become refreshingly cold in the refrigerator, add the orange and lemon and refine with the juice of the lime. Serve the iced tea with 2 ice cubes per glass.

NOTES

Closing words

Thank you so much for choosing my book.

I hope you got some ideas and inspiration.

I hope you enjoy cooking more and would be very happy if you recommend this book to your friends, family and loved ones. Feel free to leave me feedback via a review.

Yours, Clara de Vries

I'm also on Instagram and post inspiring food pictures every day.

You can find me at　　◉ **clara_de_food**

Clara De Vries

Legal

Imprint
1st edition 2021
Clara de Vries is represented by:
Contact: Daniel Schneider/ Vollersdorfer Str. 56 A/ 07548 Gera

All rights reserved.
Reproduction in whole or in part is prohibited.
No part of this work may be reproduced, duplicated or distributed in any form without the written permission of the author.

Liability for external links
The book contains links to external websites of third parties over whose content the author has no influence. Therefore, no liability can be assumed for the content of external websites. The respective provider or operator of the website is responsible for the content of the linked websites. The linked pages were checked for possible legal violations at the time of linking. Illegal contents were not recognisable at the time of linking. However, a permanent control of the contents of the linked websites is not reasonable without concrete indications of an infringement. Such links will be removed immediately if infringements of the law become known.

Printed in Great Britain
by Amazon